# THE BROADVIEW BOOK OF

# Common Errors
# in English

## ESL EDITION

# THE BROADVIEW BOOK OF

# Common Errors
# in English

## ESL EDITION

## MARTIN BOYNE
## & DON LEPAN

broadview press

**Canadian Cataloguing in Publication Data**

Boyne, Martin, 1968–    .

Common errors in English: ESL edition

ISBN 1–55111–008–3

1. English language – Errors of usage.  2. English language – Errors of usage –
Problems, exercises, etc.  3. English language – Textbooks for
second language learners. *  T. LePan, Don, 1954–    .

PE1460.B69 1993      428.2'4    C93–093161–0

broadview press
Post Office Box 1243, Peterborough, Ontario, Canada. K9J 7H5

In the United States of America:
269 Portage Road, Lewiston, New York, USA 14092

In the United Kingdom:
c/o Drake Marketing Services,
Market Place, Deddington, Banbury, Oxford, UK. OX15 0SF

Broadview Press gratefully acknowledges the support of the Canada Council, the Ontario
Arts Council, and the Ontario Publishing Centre.

Printed in Canada

1 2 3 4 5 6 7 8 9 10 11

# CONTENTS

# PREFACE

As I put together the chapters for this book, I realized how lucky I was to have English as my first language. This was not inspired by any feelings that English was somehow superior to other languages, or by the knowledge that I could communicate in my native tongue practically all over the world, but rather by an increased understanding of just how difficult this language of ours is to learn. We have a complicated verb tense system, seemingly more irregular verbs than regular ones, an orthography that could easily have been created by the most proficient (and sadistic) cryptographer, and a host of idioms and all-purpose words that defy logic. Is this an attack on the English language? Far from it. Its many peculiarities enhance it, rather than detract from it. Its rich and creative lexicon is thesauruses (or is that thesauri?) ahead of its closest rivals. And its innumerable dialects, jargons, and slangs, while appearing to threaten the very language from which they sprung, are relentlessly recreating English with each passing year and generation.

This leaves the speakers of English with a daunting task. While, on one hand, they are equipped with the linguistic apparatus to master the rudiments of the language in their English-speaking environments, on the other, many fail to come to terms with the finer points of the language. This is not unexpected, and certainly not restricted to English. Perhaps it's also necessary; after all, much of the linguistic diversity so treasured by English is caused by the impracticality of all speakers attaining the same level of linguistic competence and performance. This linguistic diversity within the language, coupled with a need to re-address the fundamental grammar that is often ignored in other areas of society, inspired this book's parent volume, *Common Errors in English*, now in its second edition.

The inspiration for the present tome came from that same notion of linguistic diversity. This time, however, it is external diversity—or, rather, countless external diversities—which is its driving force. Speakers of other languages arrive on the threshold of English with rich and varied skills, some of which will be helpful, some a hindrance. As a group, they have conflicting ideas on word order, on negative particles, on sequencing of tenses; in fact, they have conflicting ideas on just about everything, and they are forced to adjust what they know to accommodate the nuances of English. Yet what they all possess—and this, aside from their enthusiasm and tenacity, is probably their greatest asset—is an understanding of grammar and its many idiosyncrasies. The level of linguistic awareness that speakers of other languages have separate them from speakers of English perhaps more than the linguistic diversity itself. This is not to belittle my fellow English speakers, but rather to demonstrate how amazingly accessible English becomes when learners have these skills.

A love of language inspired this book as much as a desire to help ESL learners. It was an opportunity for me to look at my own language, ask myself what I knew, look up what I didn't, apply my linguistic background to it, and shape it into its present form. The book is structured in much the same way as its predecessor; in fact, some sections needed no adjustment. What is different is the approach to many of the grammatical explanations, which has been changed to stress the distinction between first-language errors (caused by factors too numerous to mention here, but including social and cultural environment, and the media) and second-language errors (usually caused by grammatical confusion between first and other language or by analogy with another rule). As the Table of Contents indicates, the emphasis is on grammar, usage, and meaning. We do not deal with idiomatic or colloquial English to any great extent, simply because it does not fit with the overall aims of the book, and because many authors before us have covered the subject admirably.

And now a few words on who can use the book and how they can use it. It is designed primarily for the student and teacher of E.S.L., but can also be used by speakers of the language who are past the actual learning stage but who still need a resource guide or some additional practice. Similarly, the book can be used by teachers who work with E.S.L. students in other subjects in order to assess their needs and identify their problems. Students from senior high school up to college and beyond, can benefit equally from the contents. While *Common Errors* can be employed as a reference guide, it can also, surprisingly enough, be read like a normal book. Many of the chapters incorporate passages of text with examples in a wrong/right format, with occasional recourse to a table or list. The exercises that come at the end are designed to deal exclusively with one particular grammatical point or aspect of usage raised by the book, often with specific reference to a particular language or language group. There is an answer key to complement the exercises. Teachers, of course, can modify or add to the exercises as they feel appropriate.

Since it is normal to do so at this stage of a preface, I should express my thanks to certain people. I wouldn't be doing this if it were not for the trust and faith placed in me by Don LePan and everyone at Broadview Press; in addition, I must thank Bill Hunter who turned what I thought would be an "occasional bit of editing" into this major project. Cheers also to Lucille for her support and understanding. Finally, for putting up with endless evenings of clicking on the keyboard, and for simply being there for me to share my joys and frustrations, thanks must go to my Mum, Anne, and to Maggie, who also gets Exercise 52 in her honour.

Martin Boyne

Peterborough, March 1993

# VERBS

The verb in English is perhaps the most confusing part of speech for second language learners. The verb can be used in several tenses, and the difference between one tense and another is often very subtle. Also, the verb is frequently composed of two or more words: equally challenging to second language learners are the order of the words and the choice of the words themselves.

# Tenses

**Simple present tense** The simple present tense poses few difficulties in regular verbs, since the verb stem or infinitive form is used for all persons, with the simple addition of -s in the third person singular.

> **Wrong:** I read books, but he read magazines.
> **Right:** I read books, but he **reads** magazines.

It is not particularly difficult to ensure that the subject agrees with the verb in sentences such as this, but even native English speakers have trouble with verb agreement when the subject and verb are separated by a long phrase or clause.

> **Wrong:** The state of Afghanistan's roads reflect the chaotic situation.
> **Right:** The state of Afghanistan's roads **reflects** the chaotic situation.

Sometimes a long sentence can in itself throw off a writer's sense of subject-verb agreement, even if subject and verb are close together. In the following example the close proximity of the subject "simplifications" to the verb has not prevented error:

> **Wrong:** The decline in the quality of American leadership is mirrored in the crude simplifications which characterise**s** the average American's view of the world.
> (*The Guardian*, April 19, 1987)
> **Right:** The decline in the quality of American leadership is mirrored in the crude simplifications which characterise the average American's view of the world.

Irregularities in verbs show up in past tense forms more than anywhere else (see below), but there are a couple of present tense irregularities to watch out for. The third person singular form of "do" and "go" are "does" and "goes," which, to add to the confusion, are not even pronounced in the same way. Another common verb, "have," is also irregular in the third person singular: be sure to use "has" instead of "haves." As in most languages, the verb "be" is most irregular:

| | |
|---|---|
| I **am** | we **are** |
| you **are** | you **are** |
| he/she/it **is** | they **are** |

**Continuous or progressive tenses** (past, present, and future) are quite unique to English. Each tense in English has a progressive equivalent; the difference in meaning is very important. "I read books," for example, is a statement which presents a general fact; by contrast, "I am reading a book" shows that the action is going on at the present time.

There are times when the simple tense must be used when the progressive tense is not permitted:

**Wrong:** Every Saturday, I am playing football and visiting my friend.
**Right:** Every Saturday, I **play** football and **visit** my friend.

**Wrong:** Each day, he is drinking coffee on his way to work.
**Right:** Each day, he **drinks** coffee on his way to work.

When a general expression of time is used, as above, the progressive tense cannot be used because it would imply one specific time. In a similar way, a question which asks what you typically or usually do is not time-specific, and the answer requires a simple tense:

**Wrong:** What do you do to relax? I am listening to music.
**Right:** What do you do to relax? I **listen** to music.

As you might expect, progressive tenses have their place too, and at certain times simple tenses must not be used. Again, when a specific time, as opposed to a general state, is indicated, a progressive tense must be used. Look at the following responses to the question "What were you doing when I called?"

**Wrong:** I watched television and read a book.
**Right:** I **was watching** television and **reading** a book.

The wrong answer suggests that these actions were suddenly undertaken and completed when the caller made the call; it is obviously ridiculous. Look for clues in the question: if it is phrased with a progressive tense, the response should be in a progressive tense.

While the use of the progressive usually indicates a specific time as opposed to a general state, it can also be used to suggest habitual or repeated action. We discovered above that "Each day he is drinking coffee on his way to work" is wrong because "each day" refers to a general time period. However, if the time adverb were changed to "these days," the progressive tense is quite acceptable:

> **Right:** These days he **is drinking** coffee on his way to work.
> **Right:** In my university days I **was reading** three books a week.
> **Or:** In my university days I **read** three books a week.

In some cases, a progressive tense is used to help define the real meaning or the specific context of the statement:

> **Right:** Next week I **will write** my English exam. (at some point)
> **Right:** Next week (at this time) I will be writing my English exam.

Each sentence has a different meaning. Note that the addition of "at this time" could only be possible in the second sentence because the progressive tense allows this specific time reference.

Ambiguity can sometimes arise when a simple tense and progressive tense are confused. It is not that one tense is wrong and another right grammatically, but purely that in the context, each has a different meaning. For instance, if someone wondered why you always asked for things to be repeated, you could respond as follows:

> **Context 1:** I have difficulty hearing.
> **Context 2:** I am having difficulty hearing (you).

Context 1 suggests general deafness, while context 2 is more likely to be limited to this particular situation.

The progressive tenses are not usually used with many verbs which have to do with feelings, emotions, or senses. Some of these verbs are: to see, to hear, to understand, to believe, to know, to think (meaning believe), to trust, to comprehend, to mean, to doubt, to suppose, to wish, to want, to love, to desire, to prefer, to dislike, to hate. Such verbs express ideas which cannot be progressive in nature; they cannot convey actions in progress.

> **Wrong:** He was not understanding what I meant.
> **Right:** He **did not understand** what I meant.

> **Wrong:** Now, the people are disliking the politicians; if the new tax becomes law, they will be hating them.
> **Right:** Now, the people **dislike** the politicians; if the new tax becomes law, they will **hate** them.

**Past Tenses** There are three tenses which express ideas in the past: the present perfect, the simple past, and the past perfect (or pluperfect). There are several problems associated with them. While many languages do not distinguish between the notion of present perfect and simple past, the distinction in English is extremely important.

**Wrong:** So far this year I signed three new contracts.
**Right:** So far this year I **have signed** three new contracts.

The use of the present perfect is necessary because the completed action is being described in the present. "Last year I signed three new contracts" would be correct because the action is complete and definitely in the past. Expressions of time are helpful indicators of the tense to use: when past time is stated or implied, the simple past is used; however, when an action continues into the present or is likely to be repeated, the present perfect is used.

Verbs which indicate motion are particularly problematic in this situation. Consider the following sentences:

1: Matthew ran away.
2: Matthew has run away.

In (1) there is no indication of where Matthew is (is he back?) or when this happened (Matthew, now 65, ran away when he was 6). All we know is that the action *happened* at some time in the past. However, in (2), we know that Matthew is still away, that the action took place in the past and has an impact on the present. The action is complete (he has gone), but the effect of the action is still being felt.

In the following, the poor sentence needs more detail, more context:

**Poor:** I saw the pyramids.
**Better:** I have seen the pyramids.
The poor sentence prompts the question "When?" while the better sentence makes you ask something like "And what were they like?" There is something incomplete about the first sentence, but it can be improved by adding a time phrase. In the second sentence this cannot be done.

**Right:** I **saw** the pyramids when I was in Egypt.
**Wrong:** I have seen the pyramids when I was in Egypt.

While grammatically correct, the following sentences depend on context for their correct meaning:

**Wrong:** Margaret Atwood wrote a number of books.
**Right:** Margaret Atwood **has written** a number of books.

Atwood is still alive and is likely to write more books. To make the first sentence right, an expression of time, e.g. "last year," firmly locating the action in the past, would be necessary. Compare this with the following:

**Wrong:** Shakespeare has written many great tragedies.
**Right:** Shakespeare **wrote** many great tragedies.

The action expressed in the sentence does not continue to the present, nor will it be repeated in the future, unless we believe in reincarnation: Shakespeare is dead, and what he did is in the past.

The present perfect simple or progressive tenses are also used in certain time phrases where many other languages use the present tense. This happens most frequently with "since" and "for."

**Wrong:** My wife works for the government since 1989.
**Right:** My wife **has worked** for the government since 1989.

**Wrong:** My jacuzzi is not working for three days.
**Right:** My jacuzzi **has not been working** for three days.

**Wrong:** You are reading that book since I left this morning.
**Right:** You **have been reading** that book since I left this morning.

The use of the present perfect in these sentences shows that the action began in the past and is continuing into the present. Note the use of the present perfect progressive tense in the second and third sets of sentences. The progressive is used here to show that the action is incomplete. This is often referred to as the "imperfective" aspect of the verb in other languages.

Another potential problem with the present perfect (and other perfect tenses) is the use of the simple past form instead of the past participle. Confusion arises because the two forms are often identical:

| Present/Infinitive | Simple Past | Past Participle |
|---|---|---|
| bend | bent | bent |
| buy | bought | bought |
| stand | stood | stood |
| stick | stuck | stuck |

In verbs such as these, it is as correct to use "I stuck" (simple past) as it is "I have stuck" (present perfect). However, many verbs have past participle forms which are different from the simple past.

**Wrong:** I ate an apple yesterday, but I have not ate one today yet.

**Right:**   I ate an apple yesterday, but I have not **eaten** one today yet.

**Wrong:**   If my teacher calls, tell her I've already went to school.
**Right:**   If my teacher calls, tell her I've already **gone** to school.

The converse of this error also occurs, i.e. using the past participle form for the simple past. Pay particular attention to this when using one-syllable "strong" or irregular verbs (those which undergo a sound change in the past forms).

**Wrong:**   The couple swum in a lake where they thought they'd be alone.
**Right:**   The couple **swam** in a lake where they thought they'd be alone.

**Wrong:**   You sung that song very well. Of course, I have sang it better.
**Right:**   You **sang** that song very well. Of course, I have **sung** it better.

The **simple past tense** is used to refer to an action that was begun in the past and completed in the past. It is the "perfective" aspect of the verb, while the **past progressive** is used to refer to "imperfect" or incomplete actions, or to ongoing actions in the same way as the present progressive.

**Wrong:**   We walked down the street when the earthquake struck.
**Right:**   We **were walking** down the street when the earthquake struck.

**Wrong:**   When the earthquake struck, we were running for cover.
**Right:**   When the earthquake struck, we **ran** for cover.

The differences between the right and wrong sentences in each of the sets above are quite subtle and based on context and common sense, but they illustrate the distinction between the ongoing nature of the progressive and the complete sense of the simple past.

The simple present, as we saw above, can also be used to express habitual action, as in "Every day, I jog five miles." An habitual action in the past can be expressed with the simple past— "Last year, I jogged five miles every day" —or with the modal auxiliary "would." However, the use of "would" is usually restricted to actions in the relatively distant past. This makes sense, since habitual action is usually only described if some length of time has passed.

**Right:**   Four years ago, I drank six beers every day.
**Better:**   Four years ago, I **would drink** six beers every day.

**Wrong:** Yesterday, I would play my new computer game every five minutes.

**Right:** Yesterday, I **played** my new computer game every five minutes.

**But:** When I was ten, I **would play** with my computer games many times every day, but now I never think about them.

One crucial thing to remember about habitual action in the past is that, in English, it is never expressed by the past progressive unless a contrast between the past and the present is being made.

**Poor:** When Mavis was a young girl, she was flying to Brazil every November.

**Better:** When Mavis was a young girl, she **would fly** to Brazil every November.

**Or:** When Mavis was a young girl, she **flew** to Brazil every November.

**Or:** When Mavis was a young girl, she **was flying** to Brazil every November, but now she practically never goes.

The **past perfect tense** is one of the easiest tenses to remember, since all forms are the same. What is difficult is learning how and when to use it. In English, there are quite definite rules about when the past perfect tense (or "pluperfect," meaning "more than perfect") should be used. Its chief use is to show that one action in the past was completed before another action in the past began.

**Poor:** I told my parents what happened.

**Better:** I told my parents what **had** happened.

Here the happening took place at a point in the past before the telling.

**Wrong:** By the time the group of tourists left Zimbabwe, they formed a very favourable impression of the country.

**Right:** By the time the group of tourists left Zimbabwe, they **had** formed a very favourable impression of the country.

**Wrong:** When he had gone, I thought very seriously about what he said.

**Right:** When he had gone, I thought very seriously about what he **had** said.

It is common, as in the sentences above, to neglect to use the past perfect when speaking of actions that happened at different times in the past. Like the present perfect, the past perfect is used with time expressions beginning with "since" and "for."

> **Wrong:** My mother knew my father since 1962, six years before they were married.
> **Right:** My mother **had known** my father since 1962, six years before they were married.

The **simple future tense** is formed by using the auxiliary "will" and the infinitive form of the verb. There is no one-word future tense in English, although the simple present can often be used when the idea expressed is in the future:

> **Right:** In two years, I start a new training program.
> **Or:** In two years, I **will** start a new training program.
> (The simple forms can also be replaced by progressive forms.)

Note that this use of present tense for future actions can only be used to indicate pre-planned actions, commonly accepted activities, etc., as shown below:

> **Right:** Next week we read a novel, the following week we discuss it in class, and then in the spring we write an exam on it. (This course of action is a pre-ordained plan which is common, recurring, and part of a larger whole.)

> **Wrong:** Next Tuesday, I read a novel while relaxing in bed. (For this to be correct, it would have to be part of a larger, pre-conceived plan.)
> **Right:** Next Tuesday, I **will** read a novel while relaxing in bed.
> **Or:** Next Tuesday, our group **visits** the local M.P., and next Wednesday, we **attend** a press conference with the national media.

When a sentence has a main and a subordinate clause referring to actions in the future, **only the main clause is in the future tense:**

> **Wrong:** When I will be 28, I will own a house.
> **Right:** When I am 28 (**subordinate clause**), I will own a house (**main clause**).

> **Wrong:** I will go running when I will have finished the laundry.
> **Right:** I will go running (**main clause**) when I have finished the laundry (**subordinate clause**).

The auxiliary "will" has an alternative form "shall" in some cases. While it is grammatically proper to use "shall" as the first person auxiliary, and "will" for the second and third persons, "shall" is losing currency in modern English. It is more often used now as an intensifier, or in commands:

| | |
|---|---|
| **Right:** | I will not do it! |
| **Better:** | I **shall** not do it! |
| | (When there seems to be some pressure to do it) |

| | |
|---|---|
| **Right:** | You will tidy up before you leave! |
| **Better:** | You **shall** tidy up before you leave! (When the person addressed has previously refused) |

"Will," however, is often adequate, especially if it is given the appropriate emphasis; it is good to avoid "shall" unless you are comfortable with it.

The **future progressive**, like the present progressive, should be used in certain circumstances where the simple equivalent either is not good enough or conveys a different meaning. In a simple sentence (with one clause), the future progressive indicates that at that point in the future, the action will be going on, implying that the action probably started before and will continue afterwards.

    1    At four o'clock tomorrow I will build a shed. (poor)
    2    At four o'clock tomorrow I will be building a shed. (good)

(1) indicates that the action will begin at 4:00 and end soon after, and means that the activity is planned specifically for that time, while in (2) the building will be going on at 4:00, probably having started beforehand. To show the difference between the simple future and the future progressive, let's add another clause to sentence (1):

> At four o'clock tomorrow I will build a shed and I will still be building it at six o'clock.

This is clearly wrong, because the nature of the simple future is such that it implies completion of the action at 4:00. The modification "I will start to build a shed" would be necessary in our revised sentence. Consider also the following:

| | |
|---|---|
| **Poor:** | When you call, I will take a shower. |
| **Better:** | When you call, I will **be taking** a shower. |

The poor sentence means that the call is the signal for the speaker to take a shower (perhaps as a way of avoiding the caller). This might be the case, so the sentence is not in itself wrong. However, the better sentence indicates the continuous nature of the action: the taking of the shower will be happening (future progressive) when the caller calls.

The **conditional** tense is not properly speaking a tense, but rather a mood. It is used when we are speaking of actions which would happen if certain conditions were fulfilled. Here are some examples:

> If I **wanted** to go to Australia, I **would have** to fly.
>
> If I **drank** a lot of gin, I **would be** very sick.
>
> I **would lend** Joe the money he wants if I **trusted** him.

Notice that each of these sentences is made up of a main clause, in which the conditional tense "would have", "would be", etc., is used, and a subordinate clause beginning with "if", with a verb in the simple past tense ("wanted," "drank," "trusted," etc.). In all cases the action named in the "if" clause is considered by the speaker to be unlikely to happen, or quite impossible. The speaker does not really want to go to Australia: she is just speculating about what she would have to do if she did. Similarly the second speaker does not expect to drink a lot of gin: if he *did*, he *would be* sick, but he does not plan to. In the same way, the speaker of the third sentence does *not* trust Joe: he is speaking about what the situation *would be* if he *did* trust Joe. Situations like these which are not happening and which we do not expect to happen are called *hypothetical situations*: we speculate on what *would* happen "if..." but we do not expect the "if..." to come true.

If we think the "if..." *is* likely to come true, then we use the future tense instead of the conditional in the main clause, and the present tense in the subordinate "if" clause, as in these examples:

> If I drink a lot of gin, I will be very sick. (Here the speaker thinks that it is very possible or likely that he *will* drink a lot of gin.)
>
> If I want to go to Australia, I will have to fly. (Here the speaker thinks that she may really want to go.)

Notice the difference between the following two sentences:

1. If an NDP government is elected, the American administration will not be pleased. (Here the writer thinks that it is quite possible or likely that the NDP will be elected.)

2. If an NDP government were elected, the American administration would not be pleased. (Here the writer is assuming that the NDP probably will *not* be elected.)

In sentence (2), " were " is a subjunctive form, described in more detail below. Some writers mistakenly use the conditional tense or the present tense (instead of the past tense) in the "if" clause when they are using the conditional tense in the main clause.

**Wrong:** If I want to buy a car, I would look carefully at all the models available.

**Right:** If I **wanted** to buy a car, I would look carefully at all the models available. (The speaker does not want to buy a car.)

**Or:** If I **want** to buy a car, I will look carefully at all the models available. (The speaker may really want to buy a car.)

**Wrong:** If television networks would produce fewer series about violent crime, parents would allow their children to watch even more television than they do now.

**Right:** If television networks **produced** fewer series about violent crime, parents would allow their children to watch even more television than they do now.

Note that "would" appears in only one clause (the main clause).

In the sentence above concerning the NDP, "were" is used instead of the usual past tense form "was." This form represents the **subjunctive mood** in English. The subjunctive is not used to the same extent in English as it is in other languages. While it still *must* be used in certain circumstances, its use is dying out, and it certainly does not have the widespread application in English that it has in many other languages. It has three main uses:

(a) Contrary-to-fact statements

**Wrong:** If a bank was willing to lend large amounts without proper guarantees, it would go bankrupt very quickly.

**Right:** If a bank **were** willing to lend large amounts without proper guarantees, it would go bankrupt very quickly.

**Wrong:** If I was you, I'd do what she says.

**Right:** If I **were** you, I'd do what she says.

Note that this is tied very closely to the conditional mood.

(b) Requests, wishes, desires, etc.

**Wrong:** The doctor advises that he stops smoking immediately.

**Right:** The doctor advises that he **stop** smoking immediately.

**Wrong:** She asked that I am there before she closes up.

**Right:** She asked that I **be** there before she closes up.

**Wrong:** If you can't do that, God helps you.

> **Right:** If you can't do that, God **help** you.

(c) The subjunctive is also used in idiomatic expressions such as "Suffice it to say ..." and "Be that as it may, ...".

The **past conditional** tense is used in conditional sentences in which we are speaking of actions which never happened. It is used in the main clause, with the past perfect tense being used in the "if" clause.

> If I had studied harder, I would have passed. (meaning that in fact I did not study very hard, and did not pass)
>
> If Kitchener had arrived at Khartoum a day earlier, he would have saved Gordon and the rest of the British garrison force. (meaning that Kitchener did not come early enough, and was not able to prevent the 1885 massacre at Khartoum)

Some people mistakenly use the past conditional tense in both clauses of sentences such as these; remember that the past conditional should be used only in the main clause; use the past perfect in the "if" clause.

> **Wrong:** If the Titanic would have carried more lifeboats, hundreds of lives would have been saved.
>
> **Right:** If the Titanic had carried more lifeboats, hundreds of lives would have been saved.
>
> **Wrong:** If the Conservatives under Robert Stanfield would have won two more seats in the 1972 election, the course of Canadian politics in the seventies would have been very different.
>
> **Right:** If the Conservatives under Robert Stanfield had won two more seats in the 1972 election, the course of Canadian politics in the seventies would have been very different.

# Active and Passive

English, like most languages, has two voices in which the action of the verb can be expressed: active and passive. The active voice takes the form

| Subject | Verb With Tense | Object |
|---------|-----------------|--------|
| e.g. The squirrel | climbed | the tree. |

The passive voice, on the other hand, puts the object of the active sentence into subject position, changes the verb to a participial form, and makes the subject the "agent," i.e. the person/thing that does the action. It takes the following form:

| Subject | "To Be" With Tense | Past Participle | "by" | Object |
|---------|--------------------|----------------| -----|--------|
| e.g. The tree | was | climbed | by | the squirrel. |

Remember that the following must be done to make the passive sentence correct: (1) the object of the active sentence becomes the subject of the passive; (2) the verb "to be" is added in the same tense as the tense of the active verb; (3) the verb in the active sentence is made into a past participle; (4) the word "by" is added as a preposition to the agent, which was the subject of the active sentence.

The most common errors involve not using the correct tense of "be," or using an incorrect participial form.

|  |  |
|--|--|
| **Active:** | The politician had made several mistakes. |
| **Wrong passive:** | Several mistakes were made by the politician. |
| **Right Passive:** | Several mistakes **had been** made by the politician. |

|  |  |
|--|--|
| **Active:** | The cannibal ate three explorers. |
| **Wrong Passive:** | Three explorers were ate by the cannibal. |
| **Right Passive:** | Three explorers were **eaten** by the cannibal. |

|  |  |
|--|--|
| **Active:** | Poor gardeners will never grow flowers successfully. |
| **Wrong Passive:** | Flowers are never grew successfully by poor gardeners. |
| **Right Passive:** | Flowers **will** never **be grown** successfully by poor gardeners. |

# Negatives

In English, statements are made **negative** by using the word "not." However, "not" cannot always be used alone, either before or after the verb, to make a statement negative:

|  |  |
|--|--|
| **Wrong:** | I play the piano, but I not play the drums. |
| **Wrong:** | I play the piano, but I play not the drums. |
| **Right:** | I play the piano, but I **do not** play the drums. |

In the simple present and simple past tenses ("one-word tenses"), the auxiliary "do" is used with "not" to indicate negation. Compound tenses, which are formed with more than one word, like the future perfect (I will have seen) and the conditional (She would like), etc., add "not" after the first word of the verb form. So, when a verb form has only one word, the auxiliary "do" is necessary to make the negative form; otherwise, "not" alone is sufficient.

> **Wrong:** The children jumped not into the river.
> **Wrong:** The children not jumped into the river.
> **Wrong:** The children did not to jump into the river.
>
> **Right:** The children did not jump into the river.
> **Right:** The children will not jump into the river.
> **Right:** The children do not jump into the river.
> **Right:** The children have not jumped into the river.

Also remember that the tense of the statements above is reflected in the form of "to do" and not in the main verb, which returns to its infinitive form without "to."

Note: to form the negative of the verb "to be," "not" is added *after* the verb, *without* adding an auxiliary:

> **Wrong:** He does not be aggressive enough in his approach.
> **Wrong:** He not is aggressive enough in his approach.
> **Right:** He **is not** aggressive enough in his approach.
>
> **Wrong:** They did not be successful in the marketing campaign.
> **Wrong:** They not were successful in the marketing campaign.
> **Right:** They **were not** successful in the marketing campaign.

It follows that when forming progressive tenses, which use the verb "to be," the negative is formed according to the "to be" model above, e.g. "You are not being fair"; "He is not being aggressive enough in his campaign."

For more practice with other aspects of negation in English, see the separate section beginning on p. 82.

# Commands

The **imperative** mood—the form of the verb that issues commands—is very simple in the affirmative form; in the negative, however, it needs the addition of the auxiliary "to do." Therefore, to make the imperative statement "Tell them to stop talking" negative, a form of "to do" is necessary:

> **Wrong:** Tell not them to stop talking.
>
> **Wrong:** Tell them not to stop talking.
> **Right:** **Do not tell** them to stop talking.

The first sentence is completely wrong, but the second is wrong in this context:

it negates the action of the infinitive form "to stop," and not the imperative form "tell." There is a very slight difference in form here, but a significant difference in meaning.

# Questions

Turning a statement (declarative) into a **question** (interrogative) poses problems similar to those encountered in negation: in one-word tenses, an auxiliary is necessary, while in other tenses, a change in word order is required.

**Wrong:**    Writes the author many good books?
**Right:**    **Does** the author **write** many good books?

**Wrong:**    The gardener has he planted the flowers yet?
**Right:**    **Has** the gardener **planted** the flowers yet?

**Declarative:**    This example will prove my point.
**Interrogative:**    **Will** this example **prove** my point?

Just as with negation, the tense of the question is reflected in the tense of the verb "to do," and not in the tense of the main verb:

**Wrong:**    Did the soldier died a noble death?
**Right:**    Did the soldier **die** a noble death?

Questions which are formed using interrogative pronouns such as "what," "who," and "which" bring about several word order changes. Compare the following:

**Declarative:**    The best route to follow is through the mountains.

**Interrogative:**
**Wrong:**    What the best route to follow is?
**Right:**    **What is** the best route to follow?

The word order of the declarative statement returns, however, when the question is expressed in a more polite way:

**Right:**    Where is the lecture hall? (Direct)

**Wrong:**    Could you tell me where is the lecture hall?
**Right:**    Could you tell me **where** the lecture hall **is** (please)?

**Right:**    What point are you trying to make? (Direct)
**Wrong:**    Can you help us see what point are you trying to make?

**Right:** Can you help us see what point **you are** trying to make?

The same rule applies when rephrasing a question in the form of a command:

**Interrogative:** What conferences will you be attending this year?

**Imperative:**
**Wrong:** Write down what conferences will you be attending this year.
**Right:** Write down what conferences **you will** be attending this year.

In many languages, two other ways of forming questions are possible. One involves changing intonation, while the other concerns "tag questions."

An easy way of indicating that a statement is no longer a statement but a question is to change the intonation in your voice so that it rises as you reach the end of the sentence. Declarative sentences have either steady or falling intonation, while the same sentence, with rising intonation, indicates a questioning tone:

**Declarative:** The lakes are badly polluted. (Intonation falls at end)

**Interrogative:** The lakes are badly polluted? (Intonation rises gradually throughout)

Although speakers of English would understand that this second sentence represents a question—since properly phrased questions also contain a rising intonation—it is not a common practice. It would be acceptable (and very effective) if the question were being asked in response to the very same statement, as below:

**Speaker 1:** Fish stocks have been depleted recently, because the lakes are badly polluted.

**Speaker 2:** The lakes are badly polluted? (Rising intonation)

The incredulity of the questioner lends a tone of doubt or surprise to the question. In this case, the more common question "Are the lakes badly polluted?" would not be as effective.

Rising intonation also combines with "wh-" question words (like "who" and "what") to indicate this same level of incredulity.

**Speaker 1:** I am going to run naked through the streets today.
**Speaker 2:** You are going to do *what*?

The usual question, "What are you going to do?", would not carry the same amount of emphasis on the "what," which is the biggest source of amazement to speaker 2. This happens with other interrogative pronouns, too:

**Speaker 1:** My friend John is going away to a secluded cottage for the weekend with his history teacher, Mrs. Phelps.
**Speaker 2:** He's going to do *what* with *whom?*

**"Tag questions"** are words or phrases "tagged" on to the end of questions to emphasize the interrogative nature of the statement. A frequent occurrence in other languages is the use of "...yes?" or "...no?" at the end of statements with rising intonation:

You are not pleased with my performance, no?
You are pleased with my performance, yes?

Neither sentence works particularly well in English; if a tag question is necessary, it should have an "are you?" or "don't you?" form to it, as in the following examples:

You are not pleased with my performance, are you?
You are pleased with my performance, aren't you?
You will discuss this with your lawyers, won't you?
You don't want to take us to court about this, do you?

In the negative tag questions above, the use of contractions is recommended; while formal writing should not contain contractions like "don't" or "can't," tag questions are not enhanced by avoiding them:

**Wrong:** You are still having bad dreams, are not you?
**Right:** You are still having bad dreams, are you not?
**Better:** You are still having bad dreams, aren't you?

Ensure, too, that when seeking a positive response, a negative tag question is used; for a negative response, a positive tag question is required.

**Wrong:** You are going to be invited to the wedding, are you?
**Right:** You are going to be invited to the wedding, **aren't** you?

The wrong sentence, however, can be right when used in a sarcastic tone, as if to say "So you think you're going to be invited to the wedding, do you?" The speaker quite obviously believes that this is unlikely. The correct sentence, on the other hand, seeks reassurance for what is believed to be the case.

# Dangling Constructions

A present participle is an -ing word ("going", "thinking" etc.). When combined with a form of the verb "to be", participles form part of a complete verb. They can also be used in a number of ways on their own, however:

> The President felt that visiting China would be unwise at that time. (Here *visiting China* acts as a noun phrase.)

> Having taken into account the various reports, the Committee decided to delay the project for a year. (Here "having taken into account the various reports" acts as an adjectival phrase modifying the noun "Committee.")

**Dangling present participles or participial phrases:** The danger of dangling occurs with sentences such as the second example above. If the writer does not take care that the participial phrase refers to the subject of the main clause, some absurd sentences can result:

> **Wrong:** Waiting for a bus, a brick fell on my head. (Bricks do not normally wait for buses.)
> **Right:** While I was waiting for a bus, a brick fell on my head.

> **Wrong:** Leaving the room, the lights must be turned off. (Lights do not normally leave the room.)
> **Right:** When you leave the room, you must turn off the lights.

In sentences such as these the amusing error is relatively easy to notice; it can be much more difficult with longer and more complex sentences. Experienced writers are especially alert to this pitfall if they begin a sentence with a participle or participial phrase that describes a mental operation; they are wary of beginning by "considering," "believing," "taking into account," "remembering," "turning for a moment" or "regarding."

> **Wrong:** Believing that he had done no wrong, the fact of being accused of dishonesty infuriated Col. North.
> **Right:** Believing that he had done no wrong, Col. North was infuriated at being accused of dishonesty.
> **Or:** Col. North was infuriated at being accused of dishonesty; he believed he had done no wrong.

> **Wrong:** Considering all the above-mentioned studies, the evidence shows conclusively that smoking can cause cancer.
> **Right:** Considering all the above-mentioned studies, we conclude that smoking causes cancer

**Better:**   These studies show conclusively that smoking causes cancer.

**Dangling past participles** (e.g., "considered," "developed," "regarded"): The same sorts of problems that occur with present participles are frequent with past participles as well:

**Wrong:**   Considered from a cost point of view, Dome Petroleum could not really afford to purchase Hudson Bay Oil and Gas. (Dome is not being considered; the purchase is.)

**Poor:**   Considered from the point of view of cost, the purchase of Hudson Bay Oil and Gas was not a wise move by Dome Petroleum.

**Better:**   Dome Petroleum could not really afford to buy Hudson Bay Oil and Gas.

**Dangling infinitive phrases:**

**Wrong:**   To conclude this essay, the French Revolution was a product of many interacting causes. (The French Revolution concluded no essays.)

**Poor:**   To conclude this essay, let me say that the French Revolution was a product of many causes.

**Better:**   The explanations given for the French Revolution, then, are not mutually exclusive; it was a product of many interacting causes.

**Wrong:**   To receive a complimentary copy, the business reply card should be returned before June 30. (The card will not receive anything.)

**Right:**   To receive a **complimentary** copy, you should return the business reply card before June 30.

**Dangling gerund** ("of going," "in doing," etc.) **phrases:**

**Wrong:**   In reviewing the evidence, one point stands out plainly. (A point cannot review evidence.)

**Poor:**   In reviewing the evidence, we can see one point standing out plainly.

**Better:**   One point stands out plainly from this evidence.

**Wrong:**   When analyzing the figures, ways to achieve substantial savings can be discerned. (The ways cannot analyse.)

**poor**   When we analyse the figures we can see ways to achieve substantial savings.

> **better**  The figures suggest that we can greatly reduce our expenses.

# Irregular Verbs

English, like so many other languages, has a number of **irregular verb forms**; the irregularities show up mainly in the past tense forms.  Irregular verbs also tend to be the most common verbs in the language, such as "to be" and "to go."  Perhaps the most confusing thing about irregular verbs in English is that the verbs seem to delight in making us look and sound ridiculous.  Just when it seems as though one "pattern" of irregularity has been mastered, along comes another exception to throw us off track.  Although irregular verbs cannot, by definition, be categorized, a certain amount of classification can be done.  Irregular verbs can be divided into several groups:

- those which undergo sound changes in the vowel in the simple past and past participle forms, e.g. "arise-arose-arisen";
- those which change their last letter, e.g. "build-built-built";
- those which undergo no change in any form, e.g. "cost";
- those which change only in the past participle form, e.g. "beat-beat-beaten";
- those which take a "-ught" ending, e.g. "catch-caught-caught";
- those with optional forms;
- those which are completely irregular and unclassifiable.

A table with common irregular verbs can be found in Appendix A.  The inescapable fact is that all irregular verbs must be learned.  Learning them in trios like the examples above can aid the memorization process.

This section will deal with particularly challenging verbs, with contrasting pairs, and with some special cases.

**Can/may/must/shall/will:** These verbs—the modal auxiliaries—have particularly strange forms in the past.  In addition, because of their nature, most do not have a past participle form:

| Present | Simple past | Past participle |
|---------|-------------|-----------------|
| can | could | been able |
| may | might | |
| must | had to | |
| shall | should } also conditional | |
| will | would }      forms | |

**To go/To be/To do:** Perhaps the most common verbs, they are arguably the most irregular. Take care, especially with "to go," to avoid using the simple past for the past participle (see p. 13 above).

| Present/Infinitive | Simple past | Past participle |
|---|---|---|
| to go | went | gone |
| to be | was/were | been |
| to do | did | done |

Note that the simple past is the most irregular form; the past participle forms all end in an "n" sound.

**To dive:** Although not irregular, "to dive" does have an alternative simple past form which is quite controversial. "Dove" is a definite American usage, but "dived" still appears in certain areas of the U.S. In Canada, the tendency is towards "dived," although "dove" is common, despite purists' attempts to purge it from the language. Without advocating the use of one form over another, use "dived" but recognize that "dove" exists. Using "dived" also means you have one less irregular verb to learn!

## Optional forms

Some verbs have two different possibilities in the simple past and past participle forms. The choice is usually between two suffixes, -ed and -t. Which one to use is typically a matter of geographical background, although the -ed suffix tends to look more correct. The -t suffix is very common, however, because the forms are pronounced more readily with the -t sound. A few of these verbs follow:

| Present/Infinitive | Simple past | Past participle |
|---|---|---|
| to burn | burned/burnt | burned/burnt |
| to lean | leaned/leant | leaned/leant |
| to leap | leaped/leapt | leaped/leapt |
| to learn | learned/learnt | learned/learnt |
| to smell | smelled/smelt | smelled/smelt |
| to spell | spelled/spelt | spelled/spelt |

Also:

| | | |
|---|---|---|
| to light | lighted/lit | lighted/lit |

Other verbs have options, but in the cases below each form has a different meaning.

> **Wrong:** No one has been hung in Canada since 1962.
> **Right:** No one has been **hanged** in Canada since 1962.

| | | |
|---|---|---|
| **But:** | No new pictures have been **hung** in the gallery recently. |

| | |
|---|---|
| **Wrong:** | The car speeded off in a cloud of dust. |
| **Right:** | The car **sped** off in a cloud of dust. |
| **But:** | You mean to say you've never **speeded** on this road? |

**To lay/To lie:** These are often confused: you **lay** something on a table, a hen **lays** eggs, but you **lie** down to sleep at night.

| Present/Infinitive | Simple past | Past participle |
|---|---|---|
| to lay | laid | laid |
| to lie | lay | lain |

| | |
|---|---|
| **Wrong:** | The government has lain the issue to one side for now. |
| **Right:** | The government has **laid** the issue to one side for now. |

| | |
|---|---|
| **Wrong:** | I lied down and I felt better for it: why don't you lay down too? |
| **Right:** | I **lay** down and I felt better for it: why don't you **lie** down too? |

## Contrasting pairs

While irregular verbs sometimes seem to follow patterns, e.g. "shake-shook-shaken" and "take-took-taken," this patterning certainly cannot be applied as a model. Quite often, by analogy with another verb form, a wrong past form is created. The following are but a few examples:

| | | Present | Simple past | Past participle |
|---|---|---|---|---|
| a. | **Based on:** | bend | bent | bent |
| | **Wrong:** | mend | *ment | *ment |
| | **Right:** | mend | mended | mended |
| | | | | |
| b. | **Based on:** | sing | sang | sung |
| | | ring | rang | rung |
| | **Wrong:** | bring | brang | brung |
| | **Right:** | bring | brought | brought |
| | **Wrong:** | cling | *clang | clung |
| | **Right:** | cling | clung | clung |
| | **Wrong:** | sting | *stang | stung |
| | **Right:** | sting | stung | stung |
| | | | | |
| c. | **Based on:** | keep | kept | kept |
| | **Wrong:** | seep | *sept | *sept |

| | | | | |
|---|---|---|---|---|
| **Right:** | seep | seeped | seeped |

| | | | | |
|---|---|---|---|---|
| d. | **Based on:** | kneel | knelt | knelt |
| | | feel | felt | felt |
| | **Wrong:** | peel | pelt | pelt |
| | **Right:** | peel | peeled | peeled |

| | | | | |
|---|---|---|---|---|
| e. | **Based on:** | grow | grew | grown |
| | | know | knew | known |
| | **Wrong:** | show | | shewshown |
| | **Right:** | show | showed | shown/showed |

| | | | | |
|---|---|---|---|---|
| f. | **Based on** | wind | wound | wound |
| | | find | found | found |
| | **Wrong** | mind | mound | mound |
| | **Right** | mind | minded | minded |

Worthy of extra attention is the pair "to read" and "to lead." The simple past and past participle forms are pronounced with the same vowel sound, but are spelled differently, giving "read-read-read" but "lead-led-led." To add to the confusion, "red" is a colour, and "lead," when pronounced like "led," is found in pencils. All possibilities are contained within the following slightly ridiculous sentence. Practice it aloud, paying attention to the different pronounciations of "read" and "lead."

> I **read** last night that she **led** me astray using a pencil with **red lead**; did I **lead** you to **read** the same?

# Ommision of Verbs

Verbs can be omitted in English in certain circumstances. This is especially common when repetition of the verb would result in clumsiness.

| | |
|---|---|
| **Poor:** | I play more aggressively than she plays. |
| **Better:** | I play more aggressively than she does. |
| **Or:** | I play more aggressively than her. |
| | (for a discussion of "than," see the section on pronouns) |

| | |
|---|---|
| **Right:** | My sister is much taller than I am. |
| **Better:** | My sister is much taller than me. |

Note here that the verb "do" cannot substitute for the verb "be":

| | |
|---|---|
| **Wrong:** | My sister is much taller than I do. |

The verb can also be omitted when its meaning is understood.

**Right:**  My sister plays the trumpet and my brother plays the cello.
**Right:**  My sister plays the trumpet and my brother the cello.

This technique does not work in all cases. It should be avoided simply because it sounds strange and is often confusing.

**Poor:**  I ordered a coffee, my mother a tea, and my father a glass of milk.
**Better:**  I ordered a coffee, my mother ordered a tea, and my father had a glass of milk.

# Indirect Speech

A final point to be made about verbs and verb tenses is the notion of **sequence of tenses**, especially as it relates to **indirect speech**. Indirect speech is a way of reporting what was said without actually quoting the material within quotation marks or inverted commas. The following is direct speech:

She said, "My poetry collection is ready to be published next week."

When placed in indirect speech, this becomes:

She said **(that) her** poetry collection **was** ready to be published **the following week**.

Four things have been done, as indicated in bold type: an optional introductory word has been added ("that"); the personal pronoun "my" has been changed to "her"; the tense of the verb has been shifted to correspond to the sequence of tenses within the new sentence; and the time phrase has been adjusted to make sense from our new perspective.

All these changes lead quite naturally to a high risk of error, especially when dealing with personal pronouns and verb tenses:

**Direct:**  When I met him he said, "You have cheated me."

**Indirect:**
**Wrong:**  When I met him he said that you have cheated me.
**Right:**  When I met him he said that **I had** cheated **him**.

Who is being addressed in the direct speech? The same person who is reporting in the indirect speech. Therefore, the second person pronoun "you" must be changed to the first person pronoun "I." In a similar way, the first person "me" of the direct speech becomes a third person "he" in the indirect version. Because the direct speech indicates what was said at that present time, it is in the present tense; when reported, it becomes a past event. This "moving back" of tenses occurs in all direct-indirect shifts:

> **Direct:** The official said, "I have reviewed your file."
> **Indirect:**
> **Wrong:** The official said he has reviewed my file.
> **Right:** The official said he **had** reviewed my file.

A simple future becomes a "future-in-the-past," indicated by the conditional marker "would":

> **Direct:** The children asked, "Will we be home soon?"
> **Indirect:**
> **Wrong:** The children asked if they will be home soon.
> **Right:** The children asked if they **would** be home soon.

In the above sentence, because the direct speech is in the form of a question, an introductory question word "if" is needed in the indirect form. Also, the question mark is removed.

When two like pronouns are used, ambiguity can result:

> **Direct:** He said, "He is ill."
> **Indirect:**
> **Ambiguous:** He said he was ill.
> **Better:** He said John (i.e. the person's name) was ill.

The ambiguous sentence raises the question, "Who was ill?" Was it the speaker or someone else? Out of context, this is confusing, but quite often the context gives clues to the true identity of the second "he" in the indirect form.

# NOUNS

## Gender

The essential fact to know about English nouns is that they have *no grammatical gender*. That is to say, unless a noun refers to a person (who is by nature a male or female) or other animal, especially household pets, that noun is said to be neuter, without gender. This aspect of English makes its noun system slightly easier to learn, since gender does not have to be learned at the same time. Note, however, that certain impersonal nouns are given a gender, usually feminine. This applies especially to transportation vessels:

> The ship was launched to the delight of the jubilant crowd, and off **she** sailed towards the horizon.

While the neuter pronoun "it" would not be incorrect, the use of "she" in the first sentence is a convention in English (ships and boats are always feminine). The use of "she" to refer to other inanimate objects is highly colloquial; there is no need, in fact, to replace the pronoun "it" in sentences such as "It's a beautiful day today."

## Articles

Because of this lack of gender, English has only one form for the definite and indefinite **articles**. "The" is the definite article, and "a" is the indefinite article, although remember that the latter must be changed to "an" before a vowel sound. Note that this rule does not apply simply before a vowel, but before a vowel *sound*:

> **Wrong:**  An unicorn is arriving here in a hour.
> **Right:**  A unicorn is arriving here in **an** hour.

Because the first vowel of "unicorn" is pronounced "yu," the regular indefinite article is used. Similarly, as the "h" in "hour" is silent, it is the equivalent of a vowel sound. Confusion often arises with polysyllabic words beginning with an "h" sound. While "a history" and "a handful" pose no problems, some people say "**an** historical account" because the stress in the word "historical" is on the second syllable. "**A** historical account" is, nevertheless, perfectly acceptable.

Remember, too, that the choice between "a" and "an" is dependent not on the initial vowel of the noun, but on the word it immediately precedes.

| | |
|---|---|
| **Wrong:** | This is not just a bad situation, it's a impossible situation. |
| **Right:** | This is not just a bad situation, it's **an** impossible situation. |

| | |
|---|---|
| **Wrong:** | Would you like an apple? —Yes, I'd like an red apple. |
| **Right:** | Would you like an apple? —Yes, I'd like **a** red apple. |

The articles are not used in English to the same extent that they are used in other languages. Nouns can frequently stand alone without their article, especially when they are being used in a general, non-specific sense. So, unless the indefinite nature of "a/an" or the definite nature of "the" is expressly meant, the article is redundant. Look at the following passage:

> In order to use <u>English</u> correctly and gracefully, it is necessary to recognize and to practise using <u>good grammar</u>. <u>Listening</u> to <u>speakers</u> who are accustomed to speaking grammatically helps to train **the ear** to recognize <u>correct usage</u>. <u>Simple, idiomatic English</u> is desirable for both <u>writing</u> and <u>speaking</u>, but it is not effortless.

The underlined words have no article, whereas in many other languages the article would be required. "Ear" is the only word with an article, necessary because it refers to a definite object: listening does not help to train any old ear, or "ears" in general, but rather *the* ear of the listener.

Further examples follow:

| | |
|---|---|
| **Wrong:** | The flying is becoming an increasingly popular leisure activity. |
| **Right:** | Flying is becoming an increasingly popular leisure activity. |

In addition to this non-specific sense, general, unquantifiable nouns such as "happiness," "sadness," "beauty," and "freedom" should be used without an article unless a particular case is being referred to. It follows, then, that we say "Beauty is skin deep," but "The beauty of the mountains was unbelievable," since the beauty referred to in the first sentence is non-specific, while that of the second sentence is one instance of beauty as it applies to the mountains in question.

| | |
|---|---|
| **Wrong:** | The freedom is something to which all prisoners aspire. |
| **Right:** | Freedom is something to which all prisoners aspire. |

The indefinite article must be repeated when referring to more than one person or thing.

| | |
|---|---|
| **Wrong:** | When I fly, I like to take a book, magazine, and crossword puzzle with me to pass the time. |
| **Right:** | When I fly, I like to take a book, **a** magazine, and **a** |

crossword puzzle with me to pass the time.

When referring to one person or thing, the indefinite article does not need to be repeated, but it can be for effect.

**Right:** He is a gentleman, scholar, and friend.
**Right:** He is a gentleman, **a** scholar, and **a** friend.

Repetition of the definite article is less important, and it is often not done.

**Right:** When going away for any length of time, be sure to lock the windows and doors of your house.
**Right:** When going away for any length of time, be sure to lock the windows and the doors of your house.

Make sure, however, that you repeat the article when the noun it modifies is used in apposition, as in the following:

**Wrong:** The prize I received was a book, book that I'll treasure forever.
**Right:** The prize I received was a book, **a** book that I'll treasure forever.

# Plural

The formation of the **plural** in English is typically very simple, involving the addition of the suffix -(e)s to the singular form. However, there are a number of irregular plural forms, as well as some special rules governing the formation of the plural of compound words and foreign terms. Irregular plurals include such common nouns as child (children), sheep (sheep), woman (women), and mouse (mice).

Be careful, however, that the exceptions do not affect the main rules: for example, while the plural of "mouse" is "mice," the plural of "house" is still "houses," and not the non-existent "hice."

In addition, certain words ending in -f or -fe form their plural in —ves, for example: knife—knives; wife—wives; life—lives; half—halves, etc. These must be learned, however, since the rule is not applied uniformly: giraffe—giraffes; chief—chiefs; roof—roofs.

**Wrong:** The leafs fell around the chieves as they sat discussing the thiefs with their plaintives.
**Right:** The **leaves** fell around the **chiefs** as they sat discussing the **thieves** with their **plaintiffs**.

While nouns ending in -y form their plural in -ies as in diary—diaries, pony—ponies, and industry—industries, nouns which have a vowel before the -y form their plural in the usual way:

> **Wrong:** I have made many journies with my family to Kenya.
> **Right:** I have made many **journeys** with my family to Kenya.

Compound and hyphenated words usually have a noun as their root, such as "attorney-general," "father-in-law," and "court martial," as well as words like "spoonful." They form their plural by making the noun part plural, and not by adding an -s to the whole word:

> **Wrong:** My brother-in-laws were the runner-ups in the contest.
> **Right:** My **brothers-in-law** were the **runners-up** in the contest.

Words borrowed from other languages into English usually adopt the plural form which exists in the parent language. Many scientific words come from Latin or Greek, and it is conventional to use the plural forms from those languages. A quick reference table summarizes the principal forms.

| Language | Singular ending | Plural ending |
| --- | --- | --- |
| Latin | -um (datum) | -a (data) |
| | -ix (appendix) | -ices (appendices) |
| | -ex (index) | -ices (indices) |
| | -us (nucleus) | -i (nuclei) |
| | -a (vertebra) | -ae (vertebrae) |
| Greek | -on (criterion) | -a (criteria) |
| | -is (thesis) | -es (theses) |
| French | -eau (chateau) | -eaux (chateaux) |
| Italian | -o (concerto grosso) | -i (concerti grossi) |

In some instances, the foreign plural form is optional. For example, a book has "indexes" but we have economic "indices"; the same book might have "appendices" but a doctor removes several "appendixes" each year.

Certain words have particular problems associated with their singular and plural forms; some of these are described in greater detail below.

**accommodation:** The plural form is not normally used.

> **Wrong:** My family and my friend's family were both unable to find accommodations downtown.

> **Right:** My family and my friend's family were both unable to find **accommodation** downtown.

**bacteria:** A plural word; the singular is "bacterium."

> **Wrong:** There were many bacterias in the mouldy bread.
> **Right:** There were a lot of **bacteria** in the mouldy bread.

**behavior:** Although some social scientists speak of "a behavior" or of "behaviors" in technical writing, in other disciplines and in conversational English the word is uncountable (i.e. it cannot form a plural or be used with the indefinite article). Say "types of behavior," not "behaviors."

> **Wrong:** He has a good behavior.
> **Right:** His **behavior** is good.
> **Or:** He behaves well.

**brain:** One person can only have one "brain." The use of the plural to refer to the "brain" of one person (e.g., "He blew his brains out") is slang, and should not be used in formal written work.

> **Wrong:** He used his brains to solve the problem.
> **Right:** He used his **brain** to solve the problem.

**criteria:** Plural; the singular is "criterion."

> **Wrong:** The chief criteria on which an essay should be judged is whether or not it communicates clearly.
> **Right:** The chief **criterion** on which an essay should be judged is whether or not it communicates clearly.

**damage:** In its usual meaning, this noun has no plural, since it is uncountable. We speak of "damage," not "a damage," and of "a lot of damage," not "many damages." The word "damages" means money paid to cover the cost of any damage one has caused.

> **Wrong:** The crash caused many damages to his car, but he was unhurt.
> **Right:** The crash caused a lot of **damage** to his car, but he was unhurt.

**data:** Like "bacteria," "media," and "phenomena," the noun "data" is plural. The singular form, which is rarely used, is "datum."

> **Wrong:** This data proves conclusively that the lake is badly polluted.
> **Right:** These data **prove** conclusively that the lake is badly

polluted.

**media:** Plural; the singular is "medium."

> **Wrong:** The media usually assumes that the audience has a very
> short attention span.
> **Right:** The media usually **assume** that the audience has a very
> short attention span.

**money:** Some people seem to think that "monies" has a more official ring to it than "money" when they are talking of business affairs, but there is no sound reason for using this plural form in good English.

> **Wrong:** The Council has promised to provide some monies for
> this project.
> **Right:** The Council has promised to provide some **money** for
> this project.

**news:** Despite the "s," this is a <u>singular</u> collective noun. Make sure to use a singular verb with it.

> **Wrong:** Today's news of troubles in the Middle East are very
> disturbing.
> **Right:** Today's news of troubles in the Middle East **is** very
> disturbing.

**phenomena:** Plural; the singular is phenomenon.

> **Wrong:** The great popularity of 'disco' music was a short-lived
> phenomena.
> **Right:** The great populaity of 'disco' music was a short-lived
> **phenomenon**.

**police:** a <u>plural</u> noun. Be sure to use a plural verb with it.

> **Wrong:** The police is investigating the case, and hope to make an
> arrest soon.
> **Right:** The police **are** investigating the case, and hope to make
> an arrest soon.

Collective nouns such as "group," "team," "number," etc. are technically singular, although they refer to more than one person or thing. Usually, when preceded by the indefinite article "a", it is considered plural; however, when the definite article "the" is used, a singularity is implied.

> **Wrong:** A group of students has gathered around the accident.

**Right:** A group of students **have** gathered around the accident.

**Wrong:** The number of people claiming unemployment insurance this year have more than doubled; a number of them does not even try to find work.

**Right:** The number of people claiming unemployment insurance this year **has** more than doubled; a number of them **do** not even try to find work.

The noun "a lot" can be applied to countable nouns like "problems" or to uncountable nouns like "trouble." In the former case, "a lot" is considered plural; in the latter it remains singular.

**Wrong:** A lot of problems is caused by the recession.

**Right:** A lot of problems **are** caused by the recession.

**But:** A lot of trouble **was** caused by the riots.

The word "none" is also a singular word. Confusion arises because "none" is often used in a sentence with a plural in it, leading to the use of a verb in the plural:

**Wrong:** None of the books are of any help to me.

**Right:** None of the books **is** of any help to me.

**Wrong:** Remember all the suits I brought home to try? Well, none of them fit me.

**Right:** Remember all the suits I brought home to try? Well, none of them **fits** me.

Remember that "none" is a contraction of "not one," and if you substitute "not one" for "none," it would be more natural to see it as a singular:

Not one of the books is of any help to me.

Well, not one of them fits me.

The same rules apply to the word "each," which is also a singular word frequently treated as a plural:

**Wrong:** Each of the students have their own writing style.

**Right:** Each of the students **has** their (or **his/her**) own writing style.

The his/her option is not given simply to show the possibility that the third person singular form can be masculine or feminine; it also demonstrates a dilemma which English has not solved in an easy way. This problem is dealt with in the section on "Language and Gender," below.

When a group of people or animals all perform a task in common, and this action involves another noun, the noun is expressed as plural. This is a difficult concept to explain, and is best shown with some examples.

**Wrong:** When informed of the decision to close the factory, the workers all shook their head in disbelief.
**Right:** When informed of the decision to close the factory, the workers all shook their **heads** in disbelief.

**Wrong:** The dog-lover opened her front door, and all her schnauzers rushed towards her and wagged their tail.
**Right:** The dog-lover opened her front door, and all her schnauzers rushed towards her and wagged their **tails**.

The use of the singular would imply that the workers all had a common head, or that all the dogs had the same tail, both of which are highly unlikely.

# Pronouns

There are several problems associated with pronouns in English.

The **personal pronoun** system has many characteristics which make it simpler than the pronoun system of other languages. For example, there is only one "you" form which covers singular, plural, formal, and informal. Also, because of the lack of grammatical gender, as described above, all non-human nouns, and nouns without obvious gender, are covered by the pronoun "it." In addition, in the third person plural, only one form, "they," is used.

| Subject Form | Object Form |
| --- | --- |
| I | me |
| you (sing.) | you |
| he | him |
| she | her |
| it | it |
| we | us |
| you (pl.) | you |
| they | them |

As can be seen, the personal pronoun system of English is very straightforward. However, care should be taken in some areas.

Pronouns do not appear in conjunction with the nouns that they are replacing.

| | |
|---|---|
| **Wrong:** | We are both **of us** going to launch a formal complaint. |
| **Right:** | We are both going to launch a formal complaint. |

| | |
|---|---|
| **Wrong:** | Joanne and Daphne **they're** going to share the leading role. |
| **Right:** | Joanne and Daphne are going to share the leading role. |

| | |
|---|---|
| **Wrong:** | The poem I am studying **it** is very emotional. |
| **Right:** | The poem I am studying is very emotional. |

| | |
|---|---|
| **Wrong:** | Some of the money I put **it** in the bank. |
| **Right:** | Some of the money I put in the bank, (the rest I spent). |
| **Better:** | I put some of the money in the bank, (and spent the rest). |

English, then, feels that the subject of the sentence is strong enough to stand alone without repeating or adding a pronoun. This is true even when the subject of the main clause of a sentence is separated from its verb by a long relative clause:

| | |
|---|---|
| **Wrong:** | The countries which Hitler wanted to conquer in the late 1930s they were too weak to resist him. |
| **Right:** | The countries which Hitler wanted to conquer in the late 1930s were too weak to resist him. |

| | |
|---|---|
| **Wrong:** | The line that is longest in a triangle it is called the hypotenuse. |
| **Right:** | The line that is longest in a triangle is called the hypotenuse. |

When using the word "than" before a personal pronoun, there is some confusion, even among native speakers of English, about whether the subject or object form of the pronoun should be used. Officially, "than" is followed by a subject form, since the verb following the pronoun is omitted. However, the object form sounds better, and is used with increasing frequency. Either is acceptable, depending on how formal your writing is.

| | |
|---|---|
| **Formal:** | She always sleeps later than he [does]. |
| **Informal:** | She always sleeps later than him. |

There is one basic rule concerning the order of object pronouns in English: the direct object pronoun always precedes the indirect object pronoun *unless* the indirect object pronoun has no preposition.

| | |
|---|---|
| **Wrong:** | Fetch the newspaper and give to him it. |
| **Right:** | Fetch the newspaper and give **it to him**. |

**Or:**   Fetch the newspaper and give **him it**.

**Wrong:**   I picked up the ball and threw over her it.
**Right:**   I picked up the ball and threw **it over her**.

Only the prepositions "to" and "for" can be omitted; other prepositions like "over," "under," and "through" must be retained to maintain their sense.

Since the direct and indirect object pronouns are identical for any given person and number, sentences containing two consecutive pronouns of the same form are not uncommon.

**Right:**   The boys asked for the books, so I gave them to them.
(direct object "to" indirect object)

**Right:**   The boys asked for the books, so I gave them them.
(indirect object—direct object)

In sentences such as the one above, the context is clear and the double pronouns are not ambiguous. As long as this is the case, using two identical pronouns is acceptable. It is best to check on context before using them, however, and when in doubt, insert the preposition.

The definite pronoun "one" should be used when you wish to avoid repeating a noun when it follows an article. Use of a regular personal pronoun is not permissible; however, omission of the noun when modified by an adjective is very effective.

**Poor:**   Would you like to work with the woman on the left or her on the right?
**Better:**   Would you like to work with the woman on the left or **the one** on the right?

**Wrong:**   Which does he prefer? The shirt in this store or it in the store we went to yesterday?
**Right:**   Which does he prefer? The shirt in this store or **the one** in the store we went to yesterday?

**Right:**   I don't know whether to buy the red car or the green.
**Better:**   I don't know whether to buy the red car or the green **one**.

Avoid using the compound personal pronouns like "myself" and "herself" when a simple personal pronoun will do.

**Wrong:**   The meeting will be co-chaired by the president and myself.

**Right:** The meeting will be co-chaired by the president and **me**.

**Wrong:** Only George, Edna, and myself were involved in the project.

**Right:** Only George, Edna, and **I** were involved in the project.

The compound personal pronouns should be used, however, in a reflexive sense.

**Wrong:** As a special treat after losing weight, he treated him to a huge ice cream.

**Right:** As a special treat after losing weight, he treated **himself** to a huge ice cream.

In the case above, the simple use of "him" would refer to someone other than the subject of the clause; "himself" turns the action back ("reflects") onto the speaker. Reflexive pronouns can also be used for emphasis, as in "She herself repaired the roof" or "She created that sculpture herself." Using "by" before such a pronoun can be ambiguous: first, it can mean that something was done alone, and second, it can refer to an action performed independently.

**Right:** She climbed the stairs by herself. (She was alone)

**Right:** She climbed the stairs by herself. (Without any help)

Usually, the context of the action, the intonation in the voice, and the nature of the action itself will help you avoid the ambiguity.

**Possessive pronouns** are formed by adding a final -s to the possessive adjective form, *except* in the first person singular:

| Possessive Adjective | Possessive Pronoun |
| --- | --- |
| my | mine |
| your | yours |
| his | his |
| her | hers |
| our | ours |
| your | yours |
| their | theirs |

Note also that the third person masculine singular form "his" remains unchanged.

An apostrophe, which normally indicates possession, is not present before the -s. Forms such as "her's" and "our's" simply do not exist in English. Another point to make about possessive pronouns is that they are not accompanied by the definite article.

**Wrong:** Whose is the book over there? —Is it not the your's?

**Right:** Whose is the book over there? —Is it not yours?
**But:** —Is it not the teacher's?

**Relative pronouns** come in a number of forms in English: "which," "that," "who," and "whom" and "what." It can also be omitted in particular cases. Here are some easy rules for choosing relative pronouns:

- "Which" refers only to things, and can be a subject or an object; it cannot have a human antecedent.

- "That" is the most flexible of all: it can refer to a human or non-human antecedent, as a subject or object; however, it cannot have a whole clause as its antecedent.

- "Who," and its object form "whom" can only be used with human (or certain other animal) antecedents.

- For the use of "what" as a relative pronoun, see below.

- The relative pronoun can be omitted when it would have been an object, but *never* when it would have been a subject, nor when a whole clause is the antecedent.

**Wrong:** Here are the people which you asked me to invite.
**Right:** Here are the people **that** you asked me to invite.
Here are the people you asked me to invite.
Here are the people **who(m)** you asked me to invite.

In this sentence, there are really four right options: the first two are used interchangeably, and with equal regularity; "whom" is less common and more formal, while "who," which is grammatically incorrect, is becoming more and more popular as an acceptable alternative to "whom." The omission of the relative pronoun is allowed because it is in the object position.

**Wrong:** I knew the woman which was murdered by the lake.
**Right:** I knew the woman **who** was murdered by the lake.
I knew the woman **that** was murdered by the lake.

Note that the omission of the relative pronoun here, in the subject position, would give the sentence a different meaning: I knew the woman was murdered by the lake.

In the following sentence, the antecedent is a whole clause:

**Wrong:** She has won a major scholarship to McGill, that is good.
**Right:** She has won a major scholarship to McGill, **which** is good.

"Which" is the only possibility, unless the comma were replaced by a semi-colon or period: "She has won a major scholarship to McGill; that is good." In this case, "that" no longer is a relative pronoun, but a demonstrative pronoun.

The use of a comma is often vital to convey a particular meaning, a meaning which, in other languages, would be distinguished by the use of different words for the relative pronoun. When the antecedent is a whole clause, the comma is essential for the sake of clarity. This can be seen clearly below:

1. He is listening to a Mahler symphony, which is unbearable.
2. He is listening to a Mahler symphony which is unbearable.

In sentence (1), the non-restrictive use of the comma makes it clear that the unbearable thing is the act of listening to the symphony; however, in sentence (2), it is the Mahler symphony which is unbearable. The "which" of sentence (1) is the only possibility, while in sentence (2), it would be more common to use "that" as the relative pronoun. This would also amplify the restrictive nature that is presented by the omission of a comma: there is a particular Mahler symphony under discussion, and it is unbearable.

When the antecedent is a single noun, commas indicate that the relative clause is supplementary, non-essential information:

1. I take it you've come to see the painting, which is in the study.
2. I take it you've come to see the painting which/that is in the study.

The relative clause in sentence (1) is unnecessary to the conveyed meaning: the comma (and the use of "which") indicate supplementary information, almost an afterthought. In the second sentence, however, the fact that the painting is in the study is not separated from the painting itself: it could be one of many paintings available, but this one is in the study.

The verb of the relative clause agrees in number and person with the antecedent to which the relative pronoun refers. There is often a tendency, however, to use the third person singular form to agree with "who."

**Wrong:** It is I who is at fault.
**Right:** It is I who **am** at fault.

**Wrong:** Why don't you try it—you who is so clever.
**Right:** Why don't you try it—you who **are** so clever.

The relative pronoun can also be "what," when it has the meaning "that which," as in "I don't know **what** you want," and "**What** I think is not important." It suggests a hidden antecedent "that" contained within the sense of the relative pronoun. However, "what" can never be used when an antecedent is present:

**Wrong:** There is the car what I have been saving for.
**Right:** There is the car **that** I have been saving for.
**Or:** There is the car I have been saving for.

**Wrong:** I returned the shoes what made my feet hurt.
**Right:** I returned the shoes **that** made my feet hurt.

Finally, relative pronouns which have words (as opposed to clauses) as antecedents normally refer to the word that immediately precedes them. This may sometimes be difficult, especially when using the -'s form of possession, in which case the word order may have to be changed.

**Wrong:** He purchased his friend's shop, whom he had known for many years.
**Right:** He purchased the shop from his friend, whom he had known for many years.

**Wrong:** On Saturday I went to my brother's wedding, whose new wife is a senior government official.
**Right:** On Saturday I went to the wedding of my brother, whose new wife is a senior government official.

In the first example, the antecedent of "whom" is "friend," not "shop"; in the second, the antecedent must be "brother," as opposed to "wedding." These can both be deduced from the form of the relative pronoun. In the following, however, this is not possible, and ambiguity could arise:

**Wrong:** I was really impressed by the recording's quality that I got for Christmas from my aunt.
**Right:** I was really impressed by the quality of the recording that I got for Christmas from my aunt.

The antecedent of "that" could be "recording" or "quality," but in this context, only the former makes sense.

# OTHER PARTS OF SPEECH

## Adjectives

The position of the **adjective** in English, when it modifies a noun, is consistently before that noun. When there is more than one adjective, a comma is placed between the adjectives:

> **Wrong:** There are huge threatening black clouds in the sky.
> **Right:** There are huge, threatening, black clouds in the sky.

Often, however, especially when there is a close relationship between the two adjectives, the comma is omitted. In the above sentence, "threatening" and "black" are very closely linked, so the following is permissible:

> **Right:** There are huge, threatening black clouds in the sky.

In fact, in many cases the comma is completely wrong since the pause created would affect the meaning of the sentence:

> **Wrong:** A great, big man with a round, red face came in carrying a bunch of big, blue balloons.
> **Right:** A great big man with a round, red face came in carrying a bunch of big blue balloons.

"Great big" and "big blue" are considered almost as single adjectives in the above sentences, whereas "round" and "red" do not have the same close relationship.

Adjectives can follow the noun they modify if they are connected to that noun by a copulative verb like "be," "become," or "seem," or by a verb of sense and feeling like "feel," "taste," or "look."

> **Right:** There is green grass on this side of the fence.
> **Or:** The grass seems green on this side of the fence.

Adjectives of quantity like "much," "few," and "many," can only precede the noun.

> **Wrong:** The students at the football game were many.
> **Right:** There were many students at the football game.

> **Wrong:** Good reasons for my lack of punctuality are few.
> **Right:** There are few good reasons for my lack of punctuality.

There are some idiomatic phrases, however, where such uses are permissible. For example,

> **Right:** The good suggestions at the meeting last night were **few** and far-between.
>
> **Right:** However, the childish insults were **many** and varied.

Numbers cannot modify a noun that precedes them.

> **Wrong:** I would like to order opera tickets. We are four.
>
> **Right:** I would like to order opera tickets. There are four of us.

However, "We are four" could be the answer a group of children might give to the question, "How old are you, then?"

The **comparative** form of the adjective is typically formed by adding the suffix -er to the adjective, as in "nice, nicer," "strong, stronger," etc. The **superlative** form ends in -est: "nicest," "strongest," etc. Only certain adjectives, especially one-syllable adjectives, end in these suffixes; the exceptions, which have to be learned separately, fall into two categories, i.e. irregular forms, and "more/most" forms.

The two main irregular comparatives and superlatives are of the adjectives "good" and "bad." They take the forms "good-**better-best**" and "bad-**worse-worst**."

> **Wrong:** My son is bad at times, but his friend is definitely badder.
>
> **Right:** My son is bad at times, but his friend is definitely **worse**.

> **Wrong:** Which is the goodest kitten in the litter?
>
> **Right:** Which is the **best** kitten in the litter?

Two other adjectives use their irregular comparative and superlative forms to form the next category of exceptions to the -er/-est rule: "many-**more-most**," and "little-**less-least**." Usually, a word with more than one syllable forms its comparative by adding "more," and its superlative by adding "most."

> **Wrong:** This house is much comfortabler than my previous one.
>
> **Right:** This house is much **more** comfortable than my previous one.

> **Wrong:** Venice is the beautifullest city in Italy.
>
> **Right:** Venice is the **most** beautiful city in Italy.

With two-syllable words ending in -y we can use -er and est, e.g. happy-happier-happiest.

> **Wrong:** Venice is the most filthy city in Italy; Naples is more
> pretty.
> **Right:** Venice is the **filthiest** city in Italy; Naples is **prettier.**

Typically, adjectives which cannot take the -er/-est suffixes sound clumsy when the suffixes are added.

When comparing two or more things and saying that one is of lesser importance, value, size, or whatever, there is no simple suffix like -er/-est. The comparative is formed by adding "less," and the superlative by adding "least." However, to avoid this rather awkward construction when dealing with one syllable words, the comparative or superlative of the opposite can be used:

> **Poor:** This is the least high mark I have ever received on a paper.
> **Better:** This is the **lowest** mark I have ever received on a paper.

> **Poor:** It's too light! Can you dim the lights and make it less
> light?
> **Better:** It's too light! Can you dim the lights and make it **darker?**

[Note that the suffix -less *cannot* be added to indicate a comparative; -less has a different meaning, i.e. "without," and is usually used with a noun.]

One of the most common errors could have occurred in the sentence you are reading right now. A word like "common" could easily form its superlative by adding -est, giving "commonest." "Most" (or "least") cannot be used in conjunction with an adjective that is already in the superlative:

> **Wrong:** One of the most commonest errors could have occurred ...
> **Right:** One of the **most common** errors could have occurred ...
> **Or (poor):** One of the **commonest** errors could have occurred ...

The same thing applies to the comparative:

> **Wrong:** He is more happier since his wife's health improved.
> **Right:** He is **happier** since his wife's health improved.
> **Or (poor):** He is **more happy** since his wife's health improved.

When the definite article "the" is used in a phrase with a comparative or superlative adjective, the comparative form must be used when only two things or people are being compared; the superlative form is used when more than two things or people are in question:

> **Wrong:** Of my two brothers, Archie is the most intelligent.
> **Right:** Of my two brothers, Archie is the **more** intelligent.
> **But:** Of all my brothers, Edgar is the **most** successful.

# Adverbs

Adverbs are usually formed by adding -ly to the adjective, e.g. "beautiful-beautifully," "dark-darkly." There are some exceptions to this rule, of course. The adverb form for "good" is not the archaic form "goodly," but rather "well." Note that "good" is frequently, and erroneously, used as an adverb:

**Wrong:** How was your driving test? —I did good.
**Right:** How was your driving test? —I did **well**. <u>or</u> It was good.

Some other adverbs do not have the -ly suffix, nor do they need it. Adverbs like "fast," "often," and "seldom" cannot be made any more adverbial by adding -ly, as the following examples show:

**Wrong:** I seldomly run as fastly as I did today.
**Right:** I **seldom** run as **fast** as I did today.
**Or:** I **rarely** run as **quickly** as I did today.

Other adverbs can be identical to their equivalent adjectives, with either an optional or unnecessary -ly suffix. Such adverbs include "slow," "right," and "cheap."

**Wrong:** It would have been fine if you'd done it rightly the first time.
**Right:** It would have been fine if you'd done **it right** the first time.

**Wrong:** She buys and sells books very cheap.
**Right:** She buys and sells books very **cheaply**.

Note that "rightly " has two meanings: "correctly," as used above, and "justly," seen below. "Right" can only be used to convey the first sense.

**Right:** When asked to voice her opinion, she **rightly** spoke up in favour of the move.

The adverb should never be placed between a verb and its direct object. If it were, it would destroy the relationship between the action (represented by the verb) and the thing acted upon (the object). The adverb should be placed either *after* the object or *before* the verb. Note that only single adverbs in -ly can precede the verb.

**Wrong:** Slow down! You're too quickly eating your food.
**Wrong:** Slow down! You're eating **too quickly** your food.
**Right:** Slow down! You're eating your food **too quickly**.

**Wrong:** I am doing carefully my research so I can write well the essay.

**Right:** I am doing my research **carefully** so I can write the essay **well.**

**Or:** I am **carefully** doing my research so I can write the essay **well.**

This also applies to more idiomatic phrases:

**Wrong:** It is difficult to keep track of who owns what since businesses change very often hands these days.

**Right:** It is difficult to keep track of who owns what since businesses change hands **very often** these days.

# Prepositions

English speakers and learners are fortunate that **prepositions** do not govern a complicated system of cases. Words followed by a preposition are "indirect objects," as in "I gave the horse **to my sister**," or simply "objects of a preposition." Nevertheless, the reasons governing the use of one preposition over another in English often make little or no sense. What good reason is there for saying "inferior to" but "worse than"? None whatsoever, but over the centuries certain prepositions have come to be accepted as going together with certain verbs, nouns etc. There are no rules to help one learn the combinations; here are some of the ones that most commonly cause difficulty.

**agree** with someone/with what someone says; agree to do something, to something; agree on a plan, proposal, etc.

**Wrong:** The union representatives did not agree with the proposed wage increase.

**Right:** The union representatives did not agree to the proposed wage increase.

**Or:** The union representatives did not agree with management about the proposed wage increase.

**angry** with someone; angry at or about something

**Wrong:** He was angry at me for failing to keep our appointment.

**Right:** He was angry with me for failing to keep our appointment.

**annoyed** with someone; annoyed by something

**Wrong:** The professor is often annoyed with the attitude of the class.

**Right:** The professor is often annoyed by the attitude of the class.

**appeal** to someone for something

**Wrong:** The Premier appealed for the residents to help.
**Right:** The Premier appealed to the residents for help.

**apply** to someone for something

**Wrong:** I applied for the Manager to hire me.
**Right:** I applied to the Manager for a job.

**argue** with someone about something

**Wrong:** They argued against each other for half an hour.
**Right:** They argued with each other for half an hour.

**arrive** in a place/at a place (not arrive a place, except arrive home). Airlines are perhaps to blame for the error of using both "arrive" and "depart" without prepositions.

**Wrong:** He won't join the Yankees until tomorrow night when they arrive Milwaukee. (*The Globe and Mail,* April 13, 1988)
**Right:** He won't join the Yankees until tomorrow night when they arrive in Milwaukee.

**attach** two or more things (not attach together)

**Wrong:** The Siamese twins were attached together at the hip.
**Right:** The Siamese twins were attached at the hip.

**borrow** something from someone

**Wrong:** I borrowed him a pair of trousers.
**Right:** I borrowed a pair of trousers from him.

**cancel** something (not cancel out, except when the verb is used to mean "counterbalance" or "neutralize")

**Wrong:** She cancelled out all her appointments.
**Right:** She cancelled all her appointments.

**care** about something (meaning to think it worthwhile, or important to you)

**Wrong:** George does not care for what happens to his sister.

> **Right:** George does not care what happens to his sister.
> **Or:** George does not care about what happens to his sister.

**centre:** centred <u>on</u> something (<u>not</u> around something); for one thing to be centred <u>around</u> another is physically impossible.

> **Wrong:** The novel is centred around the conflict between British imperialism and native aspirations.
> **Right:** The novel centres on the conflict between British imperialism and native aspirations.

**chase** someone/something <u>away</u> for doing something; despite the way the word is misused in baseball slang, the verb *chase* with no preposition means "run after," not "send away."

> **Wrong:** Blue Jay starting pitcher Jimmy Key was chased in the fifth inning.
> **Right:** Blue Jay starting pitcher Jimmy Key was pulled from the game in the fifth inning.

**collide** <u>with</u> something (<u>not</u> against something)

> **Wrong:** The bus left the road and collided against a tree.
> **Right:** The bus left the road and collided with a tree.

**compare** <u>to</u> /compare <u>with</u>: To compare something <u>to</u> something else is to liken it, especially when speaking metaphorically (e.g., "Can I compare thee to a summer's day?"). To compare something <u>with</u> something else is to judge how the two are similar <u>or different</u> ("If you compare one brand with another you will notice little difference."). Use "compare with" when noting differences.

> **Wrong:** The First World War was a small conflict compared to the Second World War, but it changed humanity even more profoundly.
> **Right:** The First World War was a small conflict compared with the Second World War, but it changed humanity even more profoundly.

**concerned** <u>with</u> something (meaning having some connection with it, having something to do with it) and concerned <u>about</u> something (meaning being interested in it, or worried about it)

> **Wrong:** The Ministry is very concerned with the level of pollution in this river.
> **Right:** The Ministry is very concerned about the level of pollution in this river.

**conform** <u>to</u>

>**Wrong:** The building does not conform with current standards.
>**Right:** The building does not conform to current standards.
>**Or:** The contractors did not comply with current standards.

**congratulate** someone <u>on</u> something

>**Wrong:** The Opposition leaders congratulated the Prime Minister for his success at Meech Lake.
>**Right:** The Opposition leaders congratulated the Prime Minister on his success at Meech Lake.

**connect** two things/connect one thing <u>with</u> another (<u>not</u> connect up with)

>**Wrong:** As soon as he connects up these wires, the system should work.
>**Right:** As soon as he connects these wires, the system should work.

**conscious** <u>of</u> something

>**Wrong:** He was not conscious that he had done anything wrong.
>**Right:** He was not conscious of having done anything wrong.
>(Note: unlike "conscious," "aware" can be used with "of" <u>or</u> with a "that" clause.)

**consist** <u>in</u>/consist <u>of</u>: "Consist in" means to exist in, to have as the essential feature; "consist of" means to be made up of.

>**Wrong:** Success consists of hard work. (i.e. The essence of success is hard work.)
>**Right:** Success consists **in** hard work.

>**Wrong:** The U.S. Congress consists in two houses—the House of Representatives and the Senate.
>**Right:** The U.S. Congress consists **of** two houses—the House of Representatives and the Senate.

**consult** <u>someone</u> (<u>not</u> consult with someone)

>**Wrong:** She will have to consult with the Board of Directors before giving us an answer.
>**Right:** She will have to consult the Board of Directors before giving us an answer.
>**Or:** She will have to talk to the Board of Directors before

giving us an answer.

**continue** something, <u>with</u> something, <u>to</u> a place (<u>not</u> continue on)

> **Wrong:** We were told to continue on with our work.
> **Right:** We were told to continue with our work.

**convenient** <u>for</u> someone, <u>for</u> a purpose/convenient <u>to</u> a place

> **Wrong:** This house is very convenient to me; it is only a short walk to work.
> **Right:** This house is very convenient for me; it is only a short walk to work.

**cooperate** <u>with</u> someone (<u>not</u> cooperate together)

> **Wrong:** The Provinces should cooperate together to break down inter-provincial trade barriers.
> **Right:** The Provinces should cooperate with one another to break down inter-provincial trade barriers.

**correspond** <u>to</u> (be in agreement with); correspond <u>with</u> (exchange letters with)

> **Wrong:** The fingerprints at the scene of the crime corresponded with those of the suspect.
> **Right:** The fingerprints at the scene of the crime corresponded to those of the suspect.

**couple** <u>of</u> things/times/people, etc.)

> **Wrong:** Both task forces will report sometime in the future after spending a couple million dollars. (*The Globe & Mail*, March 7, 1988)
> **Right:** Both task forces will report sometime in the future after spending a couple of million dollars.
> **Or:** Both task forces will report sometime in the future after spending approximately two million dollars. (In formal writing it is best to use "two" rather than "a couple of.")

**criticism** <u>of</u> something/somebody

> **Wrong:** His criticisms against her were completely unfounded.
> **Right:** His criticisms of her were completely unfounded.

**depart** <u>from</u> a place

**Wrong:** One woman was heard saying to a friend as they departed SkyDome... (*The Toronto Star*, Nov. 29, 1989)

**Right:** One woman was heard saying to a friend as they departed from the SkyDome...

**Or:** One woman was heard saying to a friend as they left the SkyDome...

**die** of a disease/of old age; die from injuries, wounds

**Wrong:** My grandfather died from cancer when he was only forty-two years old.

**Right:** My grandfather died of cancer when he was only forty-two years old.

**different** from or to (not than)

**Wrong:** These results are different than those we obtained when we did the same experiment yesterday.

**Right:** These results are different from those we obtained when we did the same experiment yesterday.

**discuss** something (not discuss about something; no preposition is needed)

**Wrong:** They discussed about what to do to ease tensions in the Middle East.

**Right:** They discussed what to do to ease tensions in the Middle East.

**divide** something (no preposition necessary)

**Wrong:** Lear wants to divide up his kingdom among his three daughters.

**Right:** Lear wants to divide his kingdom among his three daughters.

**do** something for someone (meaning something that will help); do something to someone (meaning something that will hurt)

**Wrong:** Norman Bethune did a lot to the people of China.

**Right:** Norman Bethune did a lot for the people of China.

**end:** at the end of something; in the end (no additional preposition). "In the end" is used when the writer does not say which end he means, but leaves this to be understood by the reader. At the "end of" is used when the writer mentions the end he is referring to.

> **Wrong:** In the end of *Things Fall Apart*, we both admire and pity Okonkwo.
> **Right:** At the end of *Things Fall Apart*, we both admire and pity Okonkwo.
> **Or:** In the end, we both admire and pity Okonkwo.

**end** at a place (not end up at)

> **Wrong:** We do not want to end up at the same place we started from.
> **Right:** We do not want to end at the same place we started from.

**fight** someone or with someone (not against; fight means "struggle against," so to add "against" is redundant)

> **Wrong:** They fought against each other for almost an hour.
> **Right:** They fought with each other for almost an hour.
> **Or:** They fought each other for almost an hour.

**frightened** by something (when it has just frightened you); frightened of something (when talking about a constant condition)

> **Wrong:** He was suddenly frightened of the sound of a door slamming.
> **Right:** He was suddenly frightened by the sound of a door slamming.

**graduate** from a school

> **Wrong:** He graduated McGill in 1991.
> **Right:** He graduated from McGill in 1991.

**help doing** [i.e. be unable to refrain from doing], not help from doing

> **Wrong:** She could not help from agreeing to his suggestion.
> **Right:** She could not help agreeing to his suggestion.

**hurry** (not hurry up)

> **Wrong:** She told me to hurry up if I didn't want to miss the train.
> **Right:** She told me to hurry if I didn't want to miss the train.

**identical** with (not to)

> **Wrong:** This hotel is identical to the Holiday Inn we stayed in last

week.

**Right:** This hotel is identical with the Holiday Inn we stayed in last week.

**in**: Do not use "in" where "throughout" is meant; particularly when using such words as "whole" or "entire," be careful to use "throughout."

**Wrong:** Political repression is common in the whole world.
**Right:** Political repression is common throughout the world.

**independent** of something/someone

**Wrong:** I would like to live entirely independent from my parents.
**Right:** I would like to live entirely independent of my parents.

**inferior** to someone/something

**Wrong:** Most people think that margarine is inferior than butter.
**Right:** Most people think that margarine is inferior to butter. ("Inferior" and "superior" are the only two comparative adjectives which are not followed by "than.")

**inside** or **outside** something (not of something)

**Wrong:** Within thirty minutes a green scum had formed inside of the beaker.
**Right:** Within thirty minutes a green scum had formed inside the beaker.

**interested** in something/in doing something

**Wrong:** She is very interested to find out more about plant genetics.
**Right:** She is very interested in finding out more about plant genetics.

**investigate** something (not investigate about or into something)

**Wrong:** The police are investigating into the murder in Brandon last week.
**Right:** The police are investigating the murder in Brandon last week.

**join** someone (not join up with)

**Wrong:** Conrad Black joined up with his brother Montagu in

> making the proposal to buy the company.
>
> **Right:** Conrad Black joined his brother Montagu in making the proposal to buy the company.

**jump** (<u>not</u> jump up)

> **Wrong:** Unemployment has jumped up to record levels recently.
> **Right:** Unemployment has jumped to record levels recently.

**lift** something (<u>not</u> lift up)

> **Wrong:** I twisted my back as I was lifting up the box.
> **Right:** I twisted my back as I was lifting the box.

**lower** something (<u>not</u> lower down something)

> **Wrong:** They lowered the coffin down into the grave.
> **Right:** They lowered the coffin into the grave.

**mercy**: have mercy <u>on</u> someone; show mercy to/towards someone

> **Wrong:** We should all have mercy for anyone who is suffering.
> **Right:** We should all have mercy on anyone who is suffering.

**meet/meet with**: "Meet with" in the sense of "attend a meeting with" is a recent addition to the language. If one is referring to a less formal or less prolonged encounter, however, there is no need for the preposition.

> **Wrong:** Stanley finally met with Livingstone near the shores of Lake Victoria. (The meaning here is "came face to face with for the first time.".)
> **Right:** Stanley finally met Livingstone near the shores of Lake Victoria.

**near** something (<u>not</u> near to something)

> **Wrong:** The village of Battle is very near to the place where The Battle of Hastings was fought in 1066.
> **Right:** The village of Battle is very near the place where the Battle of Hastings was fought in 1066.

**object** <u>to</u> something.

> **Wrong:** Some people have objected against being required to wear a seat belt.
> **Right:** Some people have objected to being required to wear a

seat belt.

**off** something (<u>not</u> off of)

> **Wrong:** The man stepped off of the platform into the path of the moving train.
> **Right:** The man stepped off the platform into the path of the moving train.

**opposite:** When used as a noun, "opposite" is followed by "of;" when used as an adjective, it is followed by "to" or "from," or by no preposition.

> **Wrong:** His conclusion was the opposite to mine. (Here, "opposite" is a noun.)
> **Right:** His conclusion was the opposite of mine.

**partake** of something/ **participate** in something

> **Wrong:** They have refused to partake in a new round of talks on the subject of free trade.
> **Right:** They have refused to participate in a new round of talks on the subject of free trade.

**prefer** one thing/person <u>to</u> another (<u>not</u> more than another)

> **Wrong:** They both prefer tennis more than squash.
> **Right:** They both prefer tennis to squash.

**protest** something (<u>not</u> protest against). "To protest" means to argue against; the preposition is redundant.

> **Wrong:** The demonstrators were protesting against the Government's decision to allow missile testing.
> **Right:** The demonstrators were protesting the Government's decision to allow missile testing.

**refer** <u>to</u> something (<u>not</u> refer back to something)

> **Wrong:** If you are confused, refer back to the diagram on page 24.
> **Right:** If you are confused, refer to the diagram on page 24.

**regard**: <u>With</u> regard <u>to</u> something/ <u>as</u> regard<u>s</u> something

> **Wrong:** I am writing in regards to the balance owing on your account.
> **Fair:** I am writing with regard to the balance owing on your

           account.

**Better:**  I am writing about the balance owing on your account.

**rejoice** at something (not for something)

**Wrong:**  He rejoiced for his good fortune when he won the lottery.
**Right:**  He rejoiced at his good fortune when he won the lottery.

**repeat** something (not repeat again)

**Wrong:**  If you miss an answer you must repeat the whole exercise again.
**Right:**  If you miss an answer you must repeat the whole exercise.

**request** something *or* request that something be done (but not request for something unless one is using the noun — a request for something)

**Wrong:**  He has requested for two more men to help him.
**Right:**  He has requested two more men to help him.
**Or:**  He has put in a request for two more men to help him.

**retroactive** to a date

**Wrong:**  The tax changes are retroactive from July 1.
**Right:**  The tax changes are retroactive **to** July 1.

**return** to a place (not return back)

**Wrong:**  He wanted to return back to Edmonton as soon as possible.
**Right:**  He wanted to return to Edmonton as soon as possible.

**seek** something/someone (not seek for something)

**Wrong:**  She suggested that we seek for help from the police.
**Right:**  She suggested that we seek help from the police.

**sight:** in sight (near enough to be seen); out of sight (too far away to be seen); on sight (immediately after being seen)

**Wrong:**  The general ordered that deserters be shot in sight.
**Right:**  The general ordered that deserters be shot on sight.

**speak** to someone (when one speaker is giving information to a listener); speak with someone (when the two are having a discussion)

**Wrong:** She spoke harshly with the secretary about his spelling mistakes.

**Right:** She spoke harshly **to** the secretary about his spelling mistakes.

**suffer** from something

**Wrong:** He told me that he was suffering with the flu.

**Right:** He told me that he was suffering from the flu.

**superior** to someone/something (not than someone/something)

**Wrong:** The advertisements claim that this detergent is superior than the others.

**Right:** The advertisements claim that this detergent is superior to the others.

**surprised** at/by something: "At" is used to suggest that the person is disappointed or scandalized; unless one wishes to suggest this, "by" is the appropriate preposition.

**Wrong:** I was surprised at the unexpected arrival of my sister.

**Right:** I was surprised **by** the unexpected arrival of my sister.

**tell** someone, or tell something to someone; (**not** tell to someone)

**Wrong:** I will have to tell to him not to do it again.

**Right:** I will have to tell him not to do it again.

**But:** I told my story **to** the police.

**type** of person/thing

**Wrong:** This type carburetor is no longer produced.

**Right:** This type **of** carburetor is no longer produced.

**underneath** something (not underneath of)

**Wrong:** When we looked underneath of the table, we found what we had been looking for.

**Right:** When we looked underneath the table, we found what we had been looking for.

**until** a time or an event (not up until)

**Wrong:** Up until 1967 the NHL was a six-team league.

**Right:** Until 1967 the NHL was a six-team league.

**warn** someone <u>of</u> a danger/<u>against</u> doing something/<u>not</u> to do something

> **Wrong:** She warned me about the danger involved in the expedition.
> **Right:** She warned me **of** the danger involved in the expedition.

**worry** <u>about</u> something (<u>not</u> at something/for something)

> **Wrong:** He is always worried at what will happen if he loses his job.
> **Right:** He is always worried **about** what will happen if he loses his job.

### Prepositions in pairs or lists

If a sentence includes two or more nouns or verbs that take different prepositions, make sure to include *all* the necessary words.

> **Wrong:** The fire was widely reported in the newspapers and television.
> **Right:** The fire was widely reported in the newspapers and **on** television.

# Phrasal Verbs

A number of verbs also take prepositions; in fact, some verbs, called "phrasal" verbs, are so closely linked to certain prepositions that the verb's meaning changes significantly when the preposition is dropped or changed. Consider the verb "take," for example: depending on the preposition used with the verb, the meaning of this new phrasal or "compound" verb varies greatly.

| Phrasal verb | Meaning |
|---|---|
| take aback | shock/surprise |
| take away | subtract; remove |
| take for | identify |
| take in | include; deceive; comprehend, etc. |
| take over | assume control |
| take off | remove; (airplanes) leave the ground |
| take up | adopt; occupy; challenge |

Each of these verbs (and there are many more) forms a distinct unit of meaning; in this context, the verb and the preposition are practically inseparable. Think of these phrasal verbs not as verb-plus-preposition combinations but as single verbs in their own right. Usually, they have one-word synonyms; for example, to "bring about" means to "cause." Because of this, they are usually translated into other languages as single verbs. This is a hazard for English speakers, and can be confusing for non-English speakers trying to remember the correct preposition, a preposition which frequently seems to have come about through a random process. (Incidentally, "come about" in the previous sentence means "developed.")

Phrasal verbs act differently in various grammatical circumstances. They are different from regular verb-plus-preposition combinations when they have objects:

1. **Right:**   The visitors **took off** their shoes at the door.
   **Right:**   The visitors **took** their shoes **off** at the door.

2. **Wrong:**   The bird flew the window past.
   **Right:**   The bird **flew past** the window.

3. **Wrong:**   Gangs of youths **ran** the bridge **over**.
   **Right:**   Gangs of youths **ran over** the bridge.
   **But:**   A speeding truck **ran** the woman **over**.
   **Or:**   A speeding truck **ran over** the woman.

In example (1), "take off" is a phrasal verb, and when it takes a direct object, that object can be placed between the verb and the "preposition" in certain cases. We use the term "preposition" here very loosely, because while the word is certainly a preposition in most cases, it acts here as a "postposition" or "verbal particle." The reason for the separation of the verb from its particle is further demonstration that the particle is not a preposition.

The phrasal verb must always be split when the object is a pronoun:

**Wrong:**   Where is your diary?  Did you throw away it?
**Right:**   Where is your diary?  Did you **throw** it **away**?

**Wrong:**   My car was costing too much money so I traded in it.
**Right:**   My car was costing too much money so I **traded** it **in**.

In the above sentences, the emphasis is on the final word, i.e. the verbal particle. This demonstrates the importance of this verbal particle in establishing the meaning of the phrasal verb unit.

Returning to example (2) above, "fly past" is not a phrasal verb: it is simply a verb-plus-preposition combination. The preposition at the end of the sentence makes no sense, because in this position it ceases to serve the function of a preposition.

Example (3) is similar, but this shows another complicated aspect of phrasal verbs, i.e. that there can be two identical verb-plus-preposition units, with one being a phrasal verb, and the other a straightforward verb-plus-preposition. In the first two wrong/right sentences, "run over" means the same as to "run across": it is the verb "run" with a preposition indicating direction. The third sentence shows the phrasal verb "run over," which means to "hit (and knock down)," usually involving a car, truck, or other vehicle. To avoid ambiguity, the particle is more effectively placed after the object in this sentence.

Note also that other verbs can be formed by a compound of preposition-plus-verb. These verbs have completely different meanings from their phrasal equivalents:

> **Wrong:** After the CEO's resignation, Ian overtook the company.
> **Right:** After the CEO's resignation, Ian **took over** the company.
> **Or:** He **took** the company **over** by force.

> **Wrong:** The masked men upheld the bank.
> **Right:** The masked men **held** the bank **up.**

You "take over" the running of something, but you "overtake" a car on the highway; you "uphold" a viewpoint or a decision, but a bank is "held up."

# Final Prepositions

Another potential problem with prepositions is the dilemma over whether or not to end a sentence with one. The problem usually arises when a preposition is used in a relative clause, where the object of the preposition is omitted and expressed in the relative pronoun. For example,

> There is the man that I gave the book to.

should become

> There is the man **to whom** I gave the book.

Note that the relative pronoun "that" must become "whom" or "which" when a preposition precedes it. A common problem with this repositioning of prepositions is that they are duplicated at the end as well. Ensure that a moved preposition is not also left in its original position.

> **Wrong:** This is the biggest issue about which the two sides have been fighting about.

> **Right:**   This is the biggest issue about which the two sides have
> been fighting.

While the second versions above are correct and the more acceptable in formal written English, it is quite permissible to leave a preposition at the end of a sentence in spoken and informal English.   There is nothing grievously wrong with a sentence like "This is the biggest issue the two sides have been fighting about."

A famous remark of Winston Churchill's will help illustrate the next main point:

> This is the sort of pedantic nonsense up with which I will
> not put.

Here, apparently, the prepositions "up" and "with" have been moved to their "correct" position in front of the relative pronoun, instead of being left "dangling" at the end of the sentence.   Closer inspection reveals that "put up with" is actually a phrasal verb; in this case, the "prepositions," which are actually particles, can remain at the end:

> This is the sort of pedantic nonsense that I won't put up
> with.

The same occurs in other relative clauses containing phrasal verbs.

> **Wrong:**   She is a writer up to whom I really look.
> **Right:**   She is a writer that I really look up to.

> **Wrong:**   For what do you take me?
> **Right:**   What do you take me for?

# Conjunctions

Conjunctions are a very effective way of joining ideas, words, and sentences. They can show similarities, contrasts, reasons, or simple relationships.   There are some problems which can be encountered, however, when using conjunctions. what follows is a list of common conjunctions, accompanied by examples of usage.

**Words to connect ideas that are opposed to each other:**

All these words are used to indicate that the writer is saying two things which seem to go against each other, or are different from each other.   For example, in the sentence, "He is very rich, but he is not very happy," the fact that he is not happy is the *reverse* of what we might expect of a rich man.   The word "but" indicates this opposition of ideas to the reader.

| | |
|---|---|
| although | nevertheless |
| but | though |
| despite | whereas |
| even if | while |
| however | yet |
| in spite of | |

**although:** This word indicates that in the same sentence two things that seem to go against each other are being said. "Although" is usually used to introduce subordinate clauses, not phrases.

> Although he has short legs, he can run very quickly.

> Hume and Dr. Johnson, indeed, have a good deal in common, although Hume's attitude towards religion earned him Johnson's scorn.

Be careful not to use both "although" and "but" in the same sentence; one is enough:

> **Wrong:** Although in most African countries the government is not elected by the people, but in Zimbabwe the government is democratically elected.
>
> **Right:** Although in most African countries the government is not elected by the people, in Zimbabwe the government is democratically elected.
>
> **Or:** In most African countries the government is not elected by the people, but in Zimbabwe the government is democratically elected.

**but:** This word is usually used in the middle of a sentence to show that the two ideas in the sentence oppose or seem to oppose each other. It is also quite correct, however, to use "but" at the beginning of a sentence, if what one is saying in the sentence forms a complete clause and if the idea of the sentence seems to oppose the idea of the previous sentence.

> **Right:** The civilization of ancient Greece produced some of the world's greatest works of art and gave birth to the idea of democracy, but the Greeks also believed in slavery.
>
> **Or:** The civilization of Greece produced some of the world's greatest works of art and gave birth to the idea of democracy. But the Greeks also believed in slavery.

Experienced writers are careful not to use "but" more than once in a single sentence, or in consecutive sentences; they realize that doing so tends to confuse the reader. (It is also unwise to use any combinatiton of "but" and "however" in this way.)

**Wrong:** Chief Constable Smith said that Ryan had been legally in possession of three handguns and two rifles, but he thought it "incredible" that someone should be allowed to keep ammunition at his home. But he said any change in the firearms law was something which would not be discussed by him. (*The Guardian*, Aug. 30, 1987)

**Right:** Chief Constable Smith said that Ryan had been legally in possession of three handguns and two rifles. Smith said he thought it "incredible" that someone should be allowed to keep ammunition at his home, but he would not comment directly on whether there should be a change in the firearms law.

**despite:** This word means the same as "although," but it is used to introduce phrases, not clauses.

Despite his old age, his mind is active and alert ("Despite his old age" is a phrase; it has no verb.)

Although he is very old, his mind is active and alert. ("Although he is very old" is a clause, with "he" as a subject and "is" as a verb.)

Despite the rain, she wanted to go out to the park.

Although it was raining hard, she wanted to go to the park.

Remember not to introduce clauses with "despite."

**Wrong:** Despite that the drink tasted very strong, there was very little alcohol in it.

**Right:** Despite its strong taste, there was very little alcohol in the drink.

**Or:** Although the drink tasted very strong, there was very little alcohol in it.

**even if:** This expression is used when one is introducing a clause giving a condition. The word "even" emphasizes that the condition is surprising or unusual. Examples:

Even if I have to stay up all night, I am determined to finish the job. (Staying up all night would be very unusual.)

> Even if Bangladesh doubled its food production, some of
> its people would still be hungry. (Doubling its food produc-
> tion would be very surprising.)

**however:** This word shows that what one is saying seems to go against what one has said in the previous sentence. It should normally be placed between commas in the middle of the sentence:

> The country suffered greatly during the three-year
> drought. This year, however, the rains have been heavy.

"However" should not be used to combine ideas within one sentence, unless a semi-colon is used.

**Wrong:** Hitler attempted to conquer the Soviet Union however he was defeated.

**Right:** Hitler attempted to conquer the Soviet Union; however, he was defeated.

**Or:** Hitler attempted to conquer the Soviet Union. However, he was defeated.

**Or:** Hitler attempted to conquer the Soviet Union but he was defeated.

**Wrong:** There will not be regular mail pick-up from boxes this Friday, however regular mail pick-up will resume Saturday. (*Peterborough Examiner*, Sept. 1986)

**Right:** There will not be regular mail pick-up from boxes this Friday, but regular mail pick-up will resume Saturday.

**Or:** There will not be regular mail pick-up from boxes this Friday. However, regular mail pick-up will resume Saturday.

Note that "however" in the sense of "to whatever extent" may be used to introduce a clause: "However tired we are, we must finish the job tonight.")

**nevertheless:** Like "however," "nevertheless" is normally used to show that the idea of one sentence seems to go against the idea of the previous sentence. It should not be used to join two clauses into one sentence. Example:

> According to the known laws of physics it is not possible
> to walk on water. Nevertheless, this is what the Bible
> claims Jesus did.

**whereas:** This word is commonly used when one is comparing two things and showing how they differ. Like "although," it must begin a subordinate clause, and may be used either at the beginning or in the middle of a sentence.

**Right:** Whereas Americans are usually thought of as being loud and confident, Canadians tend to be more quiet and less sure of themselves.

**Or:** Americans are usually thought of as being loud and confident, whereas Canadians tend to be more quiet and less sure of themselves.

Any sentence that uses "whereas" must have at least two clauses—a subordinate clause beginning with "whereas" *and* a main clause.

**Wrong:** In 'The Rain Horse' a young person feels unhappy when he returns to his old home. Whereas in 'The Ice Palace' a young person feels unhappy when she leaves home for the first time.

**Right:** In 'The Rain Horse' a young person feels unhappy when he returns to his old home, whereas in 'The Ice Palace' a young person feels unhappy when she leaves home for the first time.

**while:** "While" can be used in the same way as "although." If there is any chance of confusion with the other meanings of "while," however, it is better to use "although" in such circumstances.

**Wrong:** While I support free trade in principle, I think it would hurt this industry.

**Right:** Although I support free trade in principle, I think it would hurt this industry.

**yet:** This word can be used either to refer to time (e.g., "He is not yet here"), or to connect ideas in opposition to each other. When used in this second way, it may introduce another word or a phrase, or a completely new sentence.

His spear was firm, yet flexible.

Barthes decries the language of "realism" — the pretence that one can represent on the page life as it really is. Yet it is difficult to see how following his prescriptions for an art of signs that "draw attention to their own arbitrariness" can entirely escape a tendency towards art that calls too much attention to its own surface, even art that is self-indulgent.

**Words to join linked or supporting ideas:**

| | |
|---|---|
| also | indeed |
| and | in fact |

| | |
|---|---|
| as well | moreover |
| further | similarly |
| furthermore | in addition |
| not only...but also | |

**also, as well:** These two are very similar both in meaning and in the way that they are used. It is best not to use "also" to start sentences or paragraphs. Examples:

> He put forward his simplistic credo with enormous conviction. "To do well at school," he assured us, "you must be willing to study. It is also important to eat the right foods, exercise regularly, and get plenty of sleep." While the one thing we all wanted, and none of us had managed to get, was plenty of sex.

> He put forward his simplistic credo with enormous conviction. "To do well at school," he assured us, "you must be willing to study. It is important as well to eat the right foods, exercise regularly, and get plenty of sleep." While the one thing we all wanted, and none of us had managed to get, was plenty of sex.

"Also" should not be used in the way that we often use "and"—to join two clauses together into one sentence.

**Wrong:** We performed the experiment with the beaker half full also we repeated it with the beaker empty.

**Right:** We performed the experiment with the beaker half full and we repeated it with the beaker empty.

**Or:** We performed the experiment with the beaker half full. We also repeated it with the beaker empty.

**and:** If this word appears more than once in the same sentence, it's worth stopping to ask if it would not be better to start a new sentence. Usually the answer will be yes.

**Wrong:** All my family attended the celebration and most of my friends were there and we enjoyed ourselves thoroughly.

**Right:** All my family attended the celebration and most of my friends were there too. We enjoyed ourselves thoroughly.

**as well:** To avoid repetition, do not use "as well" in combination with "both."

**Wrong:** This method should be rejected, both because it is very expensive as well as because it is inefficient.

**Right:** This method should be rejected, both because it is very expensive and because it is inefficient.

**in addition, further, furthermore, moreover:** All of these are commonly used to show that what the writer is saying gives additional support to an earlier statement she has made. An example:

> It is easy to see why many countries still trade with South Africa, despite their intense dislike of apartheid. For one thing, it is the richest country in Africa. Many of its resources, moreover, are of strategic importance.

Notice that all four expressions are often used after sentences that begin with words such as "for one thing" or "first."

**indeed, in fact:** Both of these are used to indicate that what the writer is saying is a restatement or elaboration of the idea he has expressed in the previous sentence. Notice that a colon or semi-colon may also be used to show this. Examples:

> Asia is the world's most populous continent. In fact, more people live there than in all the other continents combined.

> Asia is the world's most populous continent: more people live there than in all the other continents combined.

**not only...but also:** This combination is used to join two pieces of supporting evidence in an argument. The combination can help to create balanced, rhythmic writing, but if it is to do so it must be used carefully. Notice that it is not necessary to use "but also" in all cases, but that if the phrase is omitted a semi-colon is normally required in order to avoid a run-on sentence.

**Wrong:** Not only were the Police a commercial success, they were also among the first New Wave acts to achieve musical respectability. (*Network*, Winter 1987)

**Right:** Not only were the Police a commercial success; they were also among the first New Wave acts to achieve musical respectability.

**Or:** The Police were not only a commercial success, but also a critical one; they were among the first New Wave acts to achieve musical respectability.

**plus:** Do not use this word in the same way as "and" or "as well."

**Wrong:** For one thing, the Council did not much like the design for the proposed new City Hall. Plus, there was not enough money available to build it that year.

**Right:** For one thing, the Council did not much like the design for the proposed new City Hall. As well, there was not enough money available to build it that year.

## Words used to introduce causes or reasons:

The core of most arguments involves reasons why the writer's statements can be claimed to be true, and relationships of cause and effect. It is common to experience some difficulty at first in understanding such relationships clearly. The discussion below of the word "because" may be helpful in this respect. To begin with, though, here is a list of words that are used to introduce causes or reasons:

| | |
|---|---|
| as | for |
| as a result of | on account of |
| because | since |
| due to | |

**as:** This word can either be used to show the relationship between two events in time, or to indicate that one event is the cause of another. This sometimes leaves room for confusion about meaning (ambiguity). The following sentence is a good example:

As he was riding on the wrong side of the road, he was hit by a car.

This can mean either "When he was riding on the wrong side of the road..." or "Because he was riding on the wrong side of the road...." Unless the writer is absolutely certain that the meaning is clear, it may be better to use "while" or "when" instead of "as" to indicate relationships in time, and "because" instead of "as" to indicate relationships of cause and effect.

**because:** This word creates many problems for writers. The first thing to remember is that any group of words introduced with "because" must state a cause or reason. It must *not* state a result or an example.

In the following sentences, "because" has been wrongly used:

**Wrong:** The wind was blowing because the leaves were moving to and fro.

**Wrong:** He had been struck by a car because he lay bleeding in the road.

A moment's reflection leads to the realization that both of these sentences are the wrong way round. The movement of the leaves is the "result" of the blowing of the wind, and the man's bleeding is the "result" of his having been hit. When the sentences are turned around, they become correct:

**Right:** The leaves were moving to and fro because the wind was blowing.

**Right:** He lay bleeding on the road because he had been struck by a car.

What leads many people to make mistakes like these is the sort of question that begins, "How do you know that..." or "Prove that..." or "Show that...." The person who is asked, "How do you know that the wind is blowing?" is likely to answer wrongly, "The wind is blowing because the leaves are moving to and fro." What he really means is, "I know the wind is blowing because I see the leaves moving to and fro." That answer is quite correct, since here the *seeing* is the cause of the *knowing*. Similarly, someone who is asked to show that the man in a story he has read has been hit by a car might answer wrongly, "He had been struck by a car because he lay bleeding in the road." What he really means is, "I *know* that he had been struck by a car because I *read* that he lay bleeding in the road."

It is of course awkward to use a lot of phrases such as "I know that" and "I see that." Here are some easier and better ways of answering such questions:

The movement of the trees shows that the wind is blowing.

The fact that the leaves are moving proves that the wind is blowing.

Since the man lay bleeding in the road, it seems likely that he had been hit by a car.

**due to:** Due is an adjective and therefore should always modify a noun (as in the common phrase "with all due respect"). When followed by "to" it can suggest a causal relationship, but remember that the word "due" must in that case refer to the <u>previous</u> noun:

**e.g.** The team's success is due to hard work. ("Due" refers to the noun "success.")

It is not a good idea to begin a sentence with a phrase such as "Due to unexpected circumstances..." or "Due to the fact that...." To avoid such difficulties it is best to use "because."

**Wrong:** Due to the departure of our Sales Manager, the Marketing Director will take on additional responsibility for a short time.

**Right:** Because our Sales Manager has resigned suddenly, the Marketing Director will take on additional responsibility for a short time.

**since:** When used to introduce causes or reasons (rather than as a time word) "since" is used in essentially the same way as "because."

## Words used to introduce results or conclusions:

| | |
|---|---|
| as a result | therefore |
| consequently | thus |
| hence | to sum up |
| in conclusion | in consequence |
| it follows that... | so, and so |

**as a result, hence:** Both of these are used to show that the idea being talked about in one sentence follows from, or is the result of, what was spoken of in the previous sentence.

**Right:** His car ran out of gas. As a result, he was late for his appointment.

**Or:** His car ran out of gas. Hence, he was late for his appointment.

Notice the difference between these two and words such as "because" and "since;" we would say "Because [or since] his car ran out of gas, he was late for the appointment."

"Hence" should not be used to join two clauses into one sentence.

**Wrong:** Her phone is out of order hence it will be impossible to contact her.
**Right:** Her phone is out of order. Hence, it will be impossible to contact her.

**Wrong:** It is not the film but the advertising that is exploitative, hence pornographic.
**Right:** It is not the film but the advertising that is   exploitative, and hence pornographic.

**so:** This word may be used to introduce results when one wants to mention both cause and result in the same sentence (e.g., "Her phone is out of order, so it will be impossible to contact her"). It is usually best not to use "so" to begin a sentence, in order to avoid writing sentence fragments.

If "so" is used, "because" is not needed, and vice versa. One of the two is enough.

> **Wrong:** Because he was tired, so he went to bed early.
> **Right:** Because he was tired, he went to bed early.
> **Or:** He was tired, so he went to bed early.

## Words used to express purpose:

> in order to  so that
> in such a way as to  so as to

**so that:** When used beside each other (see also "so...that" below) these two words show purpose; they indicate that we will be told *why* an action was taken. Examples:

> He sent the parcel early so that it would arrive before Christmas.

> She wants to see you so that she can ask you a question.

The words "such that" should never be used in this way to indicate purpose.

> **Wrong:** The doctor will give you some medicine such that you will be cured.
> **Right:** The doctor will give you some medicine so that you will be cured.

> **Wrong:** Fold the paper such that it forms a triangle.
> **Right:** Fold the paper so that it forms a triangle.
> **Or:** Fold the paper in such a way that it forms a triangle.

## Words used to introduce examples:

> for example  such as
> for instance  in that

**for example, for instance, such as:** The three expressions are used differently, even though they all introduce examples. "Such as" is used to introduce a single word or short phrase. It always relates to a plural noun that has appeared just before it.

> Crops such as tea and rice require a great deal of water. (Here "such as" relates to the noun crops.)

> Several African tribes, such as the Yoruba of Nigeria and

the Makonde of Tanzania, attach a special ceremonial importance to masks. ("Such as" relates to tribes.)

"For example" and "for instance", on the other hand, are complete phrases in themselves, and are normally set off by commas. Each is used to show that the entire sentence in which it appears gives an example of a statement made in the previous sentence. Examples:

> Some crops require a great deal of water. Tea, for example, requires an annual rainfall of at least 1500 mm.

> Several African tribes attach a special ceremonial importance to masks. The Yoruba and the Makonde, for example, both believe that spirits enter the bodies of those who wear certain masks.

> Tornadoes are not only a Deep South phenomenon. In 1987, for instance, over 20 people were killed by a tornado in Edmonton, Alberta.

"For example" and "for instance" should not be used to introduce phrases that give examples. In such situations use "such as" instead.

**Wrong:** In certain months of the year, for example July and August, Penticton receives very little rainfall.

**Right:** In certain months of the year, such as July and August, Penticton receives very little rainfall.

**Or:** In certain months of the year Penticton receives very little rainfall. July and August, for example, are almost always extremely dry.

**in that:** Do not confuse with "in the way that."

**Wrong:** He is cruel in the way that he treats his wife harshly.

**Right:** He is cruel in that he treats his wife cruelly.

**Or:** He is cruel in the way that he treats his wife.

**such as:** The addition of "and others" at the end of a phrase beginning with "such as" is redundant.

**Wrong:** Teams such as Philadelphia, Boston and others have been successful with a very physical style of hockey.

**Right:** Teams such as Philadelphia and Boston have been successful with a very physical style of hockey.

**Or:** Philadelphia, Boston and other teams have been successful with a very physical style of hockey.

**Words used to indicate alternatives:**

| | |
|---|---|
| either...or | otherwise |
| if only | rather than |
| instead, instead of | unless |
| in that case | whether...or |
| neither...nor | or |

**if only:** This expression is normally used when we wish that something would happen, or were true, but it clearly will not happen, or is not true.

> If only he were here, he would know what to do. (This indicates that he is not here.)

> "If only there were thirty hours in a day..." she kept saying.

**in that case:** This expression is used when we wish to explain what will happen if the thing spoken of in the previous sentence happens, or turns out to be true. Examples:

> He may arrive before six o'clock. In that case we can all go out to dinner.

> It is quite possible that many people will dislike the new law. In that case the government may decide to change it.

Do not confuse "in that case" with "otherwise," which is used in the reverse situation (i.e., when one wishes to explain what will happen if the thing spoken of in the previous sentence does *not* happen, or turns out to be false.

**otherwise:** This word has two meanings. The first is "in other ways" (e.g. "I have a slight toothache. Otherwise I am healthy"). The second meaning can sometimes cause confusion: "otherwise" used to mean "if not." Here the word is used when we want to talk about what will or may happen if the thing spoken of in the previous sentence does not happen. Examples:

> I will have to start immediately. Otherwise I will not finish in time. (This is the same as saying, "If I do not start now, I will not finish in time.")

> The general decided to retreat. Otherwise, he believed, all his troops would be killed. (This is the same as saying, "The general believed that if he decided not to retreat, all

> his troops would be killed.")
>
> You must pay me for the car before Friday. Otherwise I will offer it to someone else. (i.e., "If you do not pay me for the car before Friday, I will offer it to someone else.")

When used to mean "if not," "otherwise" should normally be used to start a new sentence. It should not be used in the middle of a sentence to join two clauses.

**Wrong:** I may meet you at the party tonight, otherwise I will see you tomorrow.

**Right:** I may see you at the party tonight. **Otherwise** I will see you tomorrow.

## Words used to show degree or extent:

| | |
|---|---|
| for the most part | to some extent |
| so...that | too...for...to |
| such...that | to some degree |
| to a certain extent | |

**so...that:** When separated from each other by an adjective or adverb, these two words express degree or extent, answering questions such as "How far...?", "How big...?", "How much...?". Examples:

> How fat is he? He is **so** fat **that** he cannot see his feet.
>
> How large is Canada? It is **so** large **that** you need about six days to drive across it.

"So...that" is the only combination of words that can be used in this way; it is wrong to say "very fat that..." or "too large that," just as it is wrong to leave out the word "so" and simply use "that" in such sentences.

**Wrong:** She was very late for dinner that there was no food left for her.

**Right:** She was so late for dinner that there was no food left for her.

**Wrong:** Dominic speaks quickly that it is often difficult to understand him.

**Right:** Dominic speaks so quickly that it is often difficult to understand him.

**such...that:** Like "so...that," the expression "such...that" is used to express degree or extent, answering questions such as, "How big...?", "How long...?", "How fast...?". Notice the difference in the way the two are used.

> **Right:** How far is it? It is <u>such</u> a long way <u>that</u> you would never be able to get there walking.
>
> **Or:** It is <u>so</u> far <u>that</u> you would never be able to reach there walking.
> How fat is he? He is <u>such</u> a fat man <u>that</u> his trousers need to be made specially for him.
>
> **Or:** He is <u>so</u> fat <u>that</u> his trousers need to be made specially for him.

The difference between the two is of course that only *one* word is normally used between "so" and "that," whereas two or three words (usually an article, an adjective, and a noun) are used between "such" and "that." Be careful not to confuse the two, or to leave out "such."

> **Wrong:** It was a hot day that nobody could stay outside for long.
> **Right:** It was **such** a hot day that nobody could stay outside for long.

# NEGATION

Ways of forming the negative in English were discussed in the section on the verb, above. There are a few other problems which are worth mentioning before this subject is put to rest.

**double negative:** English cannot tolerate double negatives. Moreover, two negatives certainly do not make a positive.

> **Wrong:** The new student feels very insecure because he doesn't know no-one in his residence.
>
> **Right:** The new student feels very insecure because he doesn't know **anyone** in his residence.

A type of double negative is acceptable on a few occasions, however. First, negating an adjective which is already negative can have great stylistic value since it has a different meaning from a simple non-negative adjective. For example, "Malaria in tropical climates is not uncommon" has a slightly different meaning from "Malaria in tropical climates is common." The technique can often be used for humorous or satirical effect, as in "His visits to the house of ill-repute were not infrequent."

Second, a double negative verb form can sometimes be used when a particular effect is sought. An example can be found in the following dialogue:

> **A:** Why don't you like my manuscript?
> **B:** I don't not like it, I just don't think it's very good.

This cannot be used too often, however, since it sounds clumsy, but it can be effective in certain circumstances.

**neither/nor:** Neither/nor is the negative form of either/or. The words are paired because they are usually found together. Be careful not to use "nor" when "or" is sufficient—this is similar to a double negative.

> **Wrong:** She does not drink nor smoke.
> **Right:** She does not drink **or** smoke.
> **Or:** She **neither** drinks **nor** smokes.
> **Or:** She does not drink, **nor** does she smoke.

"Nor" can be used without "neither," just as "or" can be used without "either." By itself, nor continues the effect of a negative found earlier in a sentence.

> **Right:** Your job should not be considered a right to which you are entitled, or a burden from which you cannot escape.

**Better:**   Your job should not be considered a right to which you are entitled, **nor** a burden from which you cannot escape.

Be sure, on the other hand, to use "or" instead of "and" as a conjunction in a negative statement.

**Wrong:**   Moose are not found in South America, Africa, and Australia.
**Right:**   Moose are not found in South America, Africa, **or** Australia.
**But:**   Many species of wildlife can be found in South America, Africa, **and** Australia.

Note also that "neither" is a singular noun.

**Wrong:**   Neither of the sisters have ever married.
**Right:**   Neither of the sisters **has** ever married.

**hardly:** The word "hardly" is, in itself, a negative; for this reason, the addition of another negative particle would make a double negative.

**Wrong:**   The advertisers claim that you can't hardly tell the difference, but they don't know nothing.
**Right:**   The advertisers claim that you **can** hardly tell the difference, but they don't know anything (*or* they don't have any idea).

**some/any:** The indefinite pronoun "some" varies when used in a negative statement: always use "any."

**Wrong:**   I wanted to see if they had some of those new CDs I was looking for, but they didn't have some.
**Right:**   I wanted to see if they had some of those new CDs I was looking for, but they didn't have **any**.

"Any" can also be used in a positive statement in order to be less specific; in a negative statement it does not change:

I wanted to see if they had **any** of those new CDs I was looking for, but they didn't have **any**.

The same rule applies to compounds of "some," like "someone" and "something."

**Wrong:**   Husband: "I'm sure I heard something—someone must be trying to steal my roses." Wife: "You're dreaming—I can't hear something, and I don't think someone cares about your precious roses."

**Right:** Husband: "I'm sure I heard something—someone must be trying to steal my roses." Wife: "You're dreaming—I can't hear **anything**, and I don't think **anyone** cares about your precious roses."

The indefinite pronouns themselves have negative forms, "nothing" and "no-one," for example, which can often be used more concisely (but not in a negative statement, of course!). All the forms described in this section are summarized in the table below.

| Indefinite Form | Negative Equivalent | After Negative, use: |
|---|---|---|
| some (adjective) | no | any |
| some (pronoun) | none | any |
| any (adjective) | no | any |
| any (pronoun) | none | any |
| something | nothing | anything |
| anything | nothing | anything |
| someone/anyone | no one | anyone |
| somebody/anybody | nobody | anybody |
| somewhere/anywhere | nowhere | anywhere |
| sometimes | never | ever |
| somehow | in no way | in any way |

Note that "someplace" is a more colloquial form of "somewhere," and the latter should be favoured. "Some place" should be written as two words in instances like the following:

**Wrong:** I'd like to take you to someplace where we can talk in private.

**Right:** I'd like to take you **to some place** where we can talk in private.

**Or:** I'd like to take you **somewhere** where we can talk in private.

Also, the word "somewhat" is most commonly an adverb which means "to a certain degree."

**Wrong:** My friend here would like somewhat good to read on the plane.

**Right:** My friend here would like **something** good to read on the plane.

**But:** His conduct was **somewhat** arrogant.

This idea of "to a certain degree" can also be used as a pronoun, but not with the same frequency as other "some-" pronouns, e.g. "My flight was somewhat of a nightmare."

# WORD ORDER

The lack of an extensive system of cases in English to distinguish between the various parts of a sentence, i.e. subject, direct object, indirect object, etc., has definite advantages; however, the disadvantage of this system is that word order in English must be very rigid. Latin, which has a system of declensions according to grammatical case, permits a very liberal word order. All of the following mean the same, "The slave was carrying books for the boy":

> Servus libros puero portabat.
> Libros servus puero portabat.
> Puero libros portabat servus.
> Portabat puero libros servus.
> Puero servus portabat libros.

English must maintain the structure "The slave was carrying books for the boy," since any variation would result in either ambiguity or nonsense:

> The boy was carrying books for the slave. (different meaning)
> The slave for the boy was carrying books. (wrong)
> Books was carrying the slave for the boy. (nonsense)
> Was carrying for the boy the slave books. (nonsense)

The usual word order in English is S-V-O, or subject-verb-object, with little variation. Other sections of this book discuss various rules for the position of various parts of speech in English; some additional points need to be made, however, concerning certain aspects of word order.

Occasionally, changes can be made to word order for stylistic (or often humorous) effect, as in "Gone are the days of chivalry," "Neither a borrower nor a lender be," or, from the Bible, "Happy is the man who fears God." Such uses sound a little archaic, and should be avoided unless that effect is sought. More common variations in word order include the following:

**Typical:** It may be valuable experience for life, but it is not conducive to learning.

**Variant:** Valuable experience for life it may be, but it is not conducive to learning.

**Typical:** My dog has strange tastes in food: she adores carrots but has no time for bones.

**Variant:** My dog has strange tastes in food: carrots she adores but bones she has no time for.

Both versions are equally right; the second is slightly more stylistic, and the digression from usual word order calls attention to what is being said.

Here are some other words and phrases which demand special attention in terms of word order:

**both:** This word should closely precede the word to which it refers.

> **Wrong:** The television news showed Russian women lining up both to buy bread and potatoes.
> **Right:** The television news showed Russian women lining up to buy **both** bread and potatoes.
> **But:** My plan for today is **both** to sell and to buy stocks on Bay Street.

**either...or:** Again, these words should directly precede the pair of things to which they refer. The same applies to "neither...nor."

> **Wrong:** I will either pick an apple or a banana.
> **Right:** I will pick **either** an apple **or** a banana.
> **But:** I will **either** pick an apple **or** simply cut down the tree.

> **Wrong:** He will go either to New York for the holiday or remain here.
> **Right:** He will **either** go to New York for the holiday **or** remain here.
> **But:** He will go to **either** New York **or** Boston for the holiday, or he might remain here.

> **Wrong:** The experiment can either be performed with oxygen or with hydrogen.
> **Right:** The experiment can be performed **either** with oxygen **or** with hydrogen.
> **Or:** The experiment can be performed with **either** oxygen **or** hydrogen.

What follows "either" must create a balance on each side of "or." In the oxygen/hydrogen example above, the first sentence is wrong because a verb would be needed between "or" and "with hydrogen." In the first correct sentence, "with" must be repeated to maintain the balance, while in the second, "with" governs "either" so it need not be repeated.

**only:** This word should come before the word or words it refers to.

**Wrong:** She asked six people to the party only.
**Right:** She asked **only** six people to the party.

**Wrong:** He had only known her for two days when he proposed to her.
**Right:** He had known her for **only** two days when he proposed to her.
**But:** He actually **only** suggested marriage after two days—he didn't formally propose.

In the first set of sentences, "only" refers to "six," demonstrating the importance of this number. In the right sentence in the second set, "only" refers not to the verb "known," but to the length of time. Compare this with the sentence that follows, where the important information under the influence of "only" is the verb "suggest," as opposed to "propose."

**first person last rule:** When speaking about both yourself and another person (or other people), always mention the others first. The first person pronoun ("I" or "me") should come last.

**Wrong:** I and my sister decided to arrange a surprise anniversary party for our parents.
**Right:** My sister **and I** decided to arrange a surprise anniversary party for our parents.

Do not be swayed by the colloquial usage of "Me and my sister" or "My sister and me." "Me" is the object form of the first person pronoun, just like "him" and "them."

**Wrong:** Me and my partner set out to win, but the opposing team taught me and him a lesson.
**Right:** My partner **and I** set out to win, but the opposing team taught him and me (*or* us) a lesson.

For more on pronouns, see the section on Nouns.

# USAGE AND MEANING

In English, there are a number of words which present problems, either because of confusion with similar words, or because of the way words are used (and misused). This section deals with the way words are used in various contexts, and presents some examples of how some words can be mistakenly used because of similarities in sound, spelling, or meaning.

# Homonyms

A homonym is a word which sounds the same as another; quite often, the word has a similar spelling. The dangers of confusing homonyms can vary from quite minor (e.g. confusing "practice" with "practise") to the very serious, as when "proscribe" is used instead of "prescribe." It is important, however, to be clear about the correct word to use in all cases. A list of commonly confused homonyms follows.

**accede/exceed:** To **accede** means to "come to the throne," while **exceed** indicates that something is larger or greater than it should be.

> **Wrong:** In the following diagram, I will indicate how demand accedes supply.
>
> **Right:** In the following diagram, I will indicate how demand **exceeds** supply.

**accept/except:** These two words are often confused because of their similar sounds. "Accept" is a verb meaning "to receive something favourably (or at least without complaining)" Examples:

> We **accepted** the invitation to his party.

> We will have to **accept** the decision of the judge.

"Except," on the other hand, is a conjunction (or sometimes a preposition) which means "not including" or "but."

> **Wrong:** All the permanent members of the Security Council accept China voted to authorize the use of force against Iraq.
>
> **Right:** All the permanent members of the Security Council **except** China voted to authorize the use of force against Iraq.

**access/excess:** "access" is a means of entering; "excess" is an over-abundance.

> **Wrong:** The protesters burned the mansions to teach the rich a lesson about the accesses of wealth.
>
> **Right:** The protesters burned the mansions to teach the rich a lesson about the **excesses** of wealth.

**adapt/adopt/adept:** To "adapt" something is to alter or modify it; to "adopt" something is to approve it or accept responsibility for it; "adept" is an adjective meaning "skilful."

> **Wrong:** The Board adapted the resolution unanimously.
>
> **Right:** The Board **adopted** the resolution unanimously.

**adverse/averse:** "Adverse" means "unfavourable"; "averse" means "reluctant or unwilling."

> **Wrong:** The plane was forced to land because of averse weather conditions.
>
> **Right:** The plane was forced to land because of **adverse** weather conditions.

**affect/effect:** "Effect" is normally used as a noun meaning "result" (It can also be used as a verb meaning "put into effect," as in "The changes were effected by the Committee.") **Affect** is a verb meaning "cause a result."

> **Wrong:** When the acid is added to the solution, there is no visible affect.
>
> **Right:** When the acid is added to the solution, there is no visible **effect**.

> **Wrong:** "The issues that effect us here on the reserve are the same issues that effect the whole riding," Mr. Littlechild said. (*The Globe and Mail*)
>
> **Right:** "The issues that **affect** us here on the reserve are the same issues that **affect** the whole riding," Mr. Littlechild said.

**alliterate/illiterate:** "Alliterate" is a verb meaning "to use consecutively two or more words that begin with the same sound."

> **e.g.** The big, burly brute was frighteningly fat.

"Illiterate" is an adjective meaning either "unable to read" or "unable to read and write well." Those who confuse the two are sometimes, if unfairly, accused of being illiterate.

> **Wrong:** Over forty percent of the population of Zambia is

functionally alliterate.

**Right:** Over forty percent of the population of Zambia is functionally **illiterate**.

**amoral/immoral:** "Amoral" means "not based on moral standards;" "immoral" means "wrong according to moral standards."

**Wrong:** The modern reader is unlikely to share Alexander Pope's views as to what constitutes amoral behavior.

**Right:** The modern reader is unlikely to share Alexander Pope's views as to what constitutes **immoral** behavior.

**appraise/apprise:** To "appraise" something is to estimate its value; to "apprise" someone of something is to inform him or her of it.

**Wrong:** The house has been apprised at $120,000.

**Right:** The house has been **appraised** at $120,000.

**capital/capitol:** As a noun, "capital" can refer to wealth, to the city from which the government operates, to an upper case letter, or to the top of a pillar. It can also be used as an adjective to mean "most important" or "principal." "Capitol" is much more restricted in its meaning—a specific American legislative building or Roman temple.

**Wrong:** The prosecution alleged that he had committed a capitol offence.

**Right:** The prosecution alleged that he had committed a **capital** offence.

**censor/censure:** To "censor" something is to prevent it, or those parts of it that are considered objectionable, from being available to the public. To "censure" someone is to express strong criticism or condemnation.

**Wrong:** The Senate censored the Attorney General for his part in the Iran-Contra affair.

**Right:** The Senate **censured** the Attorney General for his part in the Iran-Contra affair.

**compliment/complement:** To "compliment" someone is to praise him, and a "compliment" is the praise; to "complement" something is to add to it to make it better or complete, and a "complement" is the number or amount needed to make it complete.

**Wrong:** None of the divisions had its full compliment of troops.

**Right:** None of the divisions had its full **complement** of troops.

> **Wrong:** I paid her the complement of saying that her scarf complimented her dress.
>
> **Right:** I paid her the **compliment** of saying that her scarf **complemented** her dress.

**council/counsel; councillor/counsellor:** A "council" is an assembled group of officials, and a "councillor" is a member of that group. "Counsel" is advice, or in the special case of a lawyer, the person offering advice. In other situations the person offering "counsel" is a "counsellor."

> **Wrong:** The city counsel met to discuss the proposed bylaw.
>
> **Right:** The city **council** met to discuss the proposed bylaw.

**defect/deflect:** When someone "defects," they leave a country without permission; on the other hand, when something is "deflected," it goes off course after hitting something else.

> **Wrong:** When the scientist deflected from the communist regime, his home country immediately began to worry about the consequences.
>
> **Right:** When the scientist **defected** from the communist regime, his home country immediately began to worry about the consequences.

**dependent/dependant:** "Dependent" is the adjective, "dependant" the noun. You are dependent on someone or something, and your young children are your dependants; they are dependent on you.

> **Wrong:** Emily is still dependant on her parents for financial support.
>
> **Right:** Emily is still **dependent** on her parents for financial support.

**discrete/discreet:** "Discrete" means "separate" or "distinct," whereas "discreet" means "prudent and tactful" or "unwilling to give away secrets."

> **Wrong:** Johnny Carson is not renowned for being discrete.
>
> **Right:** Johnny Carson is not renowned for being **discreet**.

**elder/older:** "Elder" can act as an adjective ("my elder son") or a noun ("The elder of the two"). "Older" can act only as an adjective. If using than, use older.

> **Wrong:** She is four years elder than her sister.
>
> **Right:** She is four years **older** than her sister.

**elicit/illicit:** "Elicit" is a verb; one "elicits" information about something. "Illicit" is an adjective meaning "illegal" or "not approved."

> **Wrong:** She has been dealing in elicit drugs for some time.
> **Right:** She has been dealing in **illicit** drugs for some time.

**eligible/illegible:** These are two words which have very different meanings: if your writing is "illegible," it cannot be read; if you are "eligible" for something, it means you are qualified. The stress in "eligible" is on the first syllable, but on the second in "illegible."

> **Wrong:** She could not receive welfare benefits because she was not illegible.
> **Right:** She could not receive welfare benefits because she was not **eligible**.

**ensure/insure:** "Ensure" can be used interchangeably with "insure" when its meaning is to "make sure," but only "insure" can be used when meaning to "safeguard" yourself against loss.

> **Wrong:** The family lost everything in the fire—it was worse because they were not ensured.
> **Right:** The family lost everything in the fire—it was worse because they were not **insured**.

**emigrant/immigrant:** "To migrate" is to move from one place to another. The prefix "ex", shortened to "e", means "out of", so an "emigrant" from a country is someone who is moving out of it. The prefix "in" or "im" means "in" or "into", so an **immigrant** to a country is someone moving into it. Similarly, "emigration" is the movement of people out of a country, while "immigration" is the movement of people into a country. Notice the spelling in both cases; e-migrant (one "m"), im-migrant (two "m"s).

> **Wrong:** More than 100,000 emigrants entered America last year.
> **Right:** More than 100,000 **immigrants** entered America last year.

**eminent/imminent/immanent:** A person is "eminent" if she is well-known and well-respected; an event is "imminent" if it is about to happen; a quality (or a god) is "immanent" if it pervades everything.

> **Wrong:** Even those working for the Ontario NDP in the 1990 campaign did not believe that a majority victory was immanent.
> **Right:** Even those working for the Ontario NDP in the 1990 campaign did not believe that a majority victory was **imminent**.

**formerly/formally:** The similarity of sound often leads to confusion.

> **Wrong:** In August Mr. Laurel formerly broke with Mrs. Aquino. (*The Globe and Mail*, Feb. 9, 1989)
>
> **Right:** In August Mr. Laurel **formally** broke with Mrs. Aquino.

**forward/foreword:** You find a "foreword" before the other words in a book.

> **Wrong:** The author admits in the forward that his research was not comprehensive.
>
> **Right:** The author admits in the **foreword** that his research was not comprehensive.

**further/farther:** "Farther" refers only to physical distance.

> **Wrong:** Eisenhower argued that the plan should receive farther study.
>
> **Right:** Eisenhower argued that the plan should receive **further** study.

**illusion/allusion:** An "allusion" is an indirect reference to something; an "illusion" is something falsely supposed to exist.

> **Wrong:** Joyce is making an illusion in this passage to a Shakespearean sonnet.
>
> **Right:** Joyce is making an **allusion** in this passage to a Shakespearean sonnet.

**incidents/incidence:** "Incidents" is the plural of "incident" (happening), whereas "incidence" is a singular noun meaning the rate at which something occurs.

> **Wrong:** The incidents of lung cancer is much lower in Zambia than it is in North America.
>
> **Right:** The **incidence** of lung cancer is much lower in Zambia than it is in North America.

**ingenious/ingenuous:** "Ingenious" means "clever;" "ingenuous" means "pleasantly open and unsophisticated."

> **Wrong:** Her manner was completely ingenious; I cannot imagine she was trying to deceive us.
>
> **Right:** Her manner was completely **ingenuous**; I cannot imagine she was trying to deceive us.

**its/it's:** Its is an adjective meaning "belonging to it." **It's** is a contraction of "it is"—a pronoun plus a verb. (Similarly, "whose" is an adjective meaning "belonging to whom," whereas "who's" is a contraction of "who is") The fact that contractions should not be used in formal writing should make it easier to distinguish between the two.

> **Wrong:** Its important to remember that the population of North America in this period was less than 10 million.
>
> **Right:** **It is** important to remember that the population of North America in this period was less than 10 million.

> **Wrong:** A coniferous tree continually sheds it's leaves.
>
> **Right:** A coniferous tree continually sheds **its** leaves.

**lightning/lightening:** One is not likely to see the sky "lightening" until after the thunder and "lightning" are over.

> **Wrong:** Three of the men were severely injured by the lightening.
>
> **Right:** Three of the men were severely injured by the **lightning**.

**loath/loathe:** "Loath" is the adjective; "loathe" is the verb.

> **Wrong:** He told me he is beginning to loath his job.
>
> **Right:** He told me he is beginning to **loathe** his job.

**loose/lose:** "Loose" is normally used as an adjective meaning "not tight;" as a verb it means "to make loose" (e.g., "He loosed the reins"). "Lose" is of course always a verb.

> **Wrong:** As soon as it became dark she began to loose control of herself.
>
> **Right:** As soon as it became dark she began to **lose** control of herself.

> **Wrong:** If this movie doesn't bring the song back to the hit parade, then you know it's flopped — and that Spielberg is loosing his touch. (*The Toronto Star*, Dec. 22, 1989)
>
> **Right:** If this movie doesn't bring the song back to the hit parade, then you know it's flopped — and that Spielberg is **losing** his touch.

**motif/motive:** A "motif" is a symbol or sign used to represent something; a "motive" is a cause or reason which "motivates" you to do something, as in "the murderer's motive."

> **Wrong:** Fire is one of the great motives of Wagnerian opera.
>
> **Right:** Fire is one of the great **motifs** of Wagnerian opera.

**pacific/specific:** Frequently confused, these two words have very different meanings. "Specific" means "particular"; on the other hand, "pacific" should refer either to an ocean or to a state of peace or calm.

> **Wrong:** Your argument is too vague; it lacks reference to pacific issues.
>
> **Right:** Your argument is too vague; it lacks reference to **specific** issues.

**pore/pour:** As *The Globe and Mail Style Book* puts it, one should "not write of someone pouring over a book unless the tome in question is getting wet."

> **Wrong:** After pouring over the evidence, the committee could find no evidence of wrongdoing.
>
> **Right:** After **poring** over the evidence, the committee could find no evidence of wrongdoing.

**predominate/predominant:** "Predominate" is the verb, "predominant" the adjective. (Either "predominately" or "predominantly" may be used as adverbs.)

> **Wrong:** The Social Credit movement was predominate only in Alberta and British Columbia.
>
> **Right:** The Social Credit movement was **predominant** only in Alberta and British Columbia.

**prescribe/proscribe:** Confusion of these two words can make a great difference to your meaning. "Prescribe" is to suggest or order something, usually with positive intention; "proscribe" is almost the opposite—it means to "condemn" or even to "ban," and certainly has no hint of positive suggestion.

> **Wrong:** The doctor made his diagnosis and proscribed some antibiotics.
>
> **Right:** The doctor made his diagnosis and **prescribed** some antibiotics.

**principal/principle:** "Principal" can be either a noun or an adjective. As a noun it means "the person in the highest position of authority in an organization" (e.g., "a school principal") or an amount of money, as distinguished from the interest on it. As an adjective it means "first in rank or importance" ("The principal city of northern Nigeria is Kano"). "Principle" is always a noun, and is never used of a person; a "principle" is a "basic truth or doctrine, a code of conduct, or a law describing how something works."

> **Wrong:** We feel this is a matter of principal.
>
> **Right:** We feel this is a matter of **principle**.

**Wrong:** Up went the shares of the two principle players in our emerging mobile telephone field. (*Financial Post*, June 12, 1989)

**Right:** Up went the shares of the two **principal** players in our emerging mobile telephone field.

**prodigy/protégé:** A "prodigy" is a genius, often referring to a child; however, you take a "protégé" under your wing in order to "protect" them. The latter is also someone in whose progress you have a special and often affectionate interest.

**Wrong:** The infamous gangster of the 1930s was unfailing in his kindness towards his prodigy.

**Right:** The infamous gangster of the 1930s was unfailing in his kindness towards his **protégé**.

**rational/rationale:** "Rational" is an adjective meaning "logical or sensible." A "rationale" is an explanation for something.

**Wrong:** The underlying rational for the proliferation of soaps and detergents is not to make our skin or clothes any cleaner, but to increase the profits of the manufacturers.

**Right:** The underlying **rationale** for the proliferation of soaps and detergents is not to make our skin or clothes any cleaner, but to increase the profits of the manufacturers.

**ravish/ravage:** "Ravish" has two quite unrelated meanings—to rape, or to fill with delight. To "ravage" is to damage or destroy.

**Wrong:** The tree had been ravished by insects.

**Right:** The tree had been **ravaged** by insects.

**simulate/stimulate:** One letter can make all the difference. To "simulate" something is to do something which is like it, or "similar" to it; however, to "stimulate" is to provoke a reaction in something.

**Wrong:** The researcher set up the test to stimulate real life.

**Right:** The researcher set up the test to **simulate** real life.

**stationary/stationery:** "Stationary" means "not moving;" "stationery" is what you write on.

**Wrong:** As Mr. Blakeney remembered it, Lord Taylor "would always park his car in the no-parking zone outside the Bessborough Hotel, leaving House of Lords "stationary" on the windshield." (*The Toronto Star*, June 1987)

**Right:** As Mr. Blakeney remembered it, Lord Taylor "would always park his car in the no-parking zone outside the Bessborough Hotel, leaving House of Lords **stationery** on the windshield." (remember that paper is a form of stationery.)

**they/their/there/they're:** Four words that are confused perhaps more frequently than any others. "They" is a pronoun used to replace any plural noun (e.g., books, people, numbers). "There" can be used to mean "in" (or "at") "that place", or can be used as an introductory word before various forms of the verb "to be" ("There is, There had been", etc.). "Their" is a possessive adjective meaning "belonging to them." Beware in particular of substituting "they" for "there":

**Wrong:** They were many people in the crowd.
**Right:** **There** were many people in the crowd.

The easiest way to check whether one is making this mistake is to ask if it would make sense to replace "they" with a noun. In the above sentence, for example, it would obviously be absurd to say, "The people were many people in the crowd."

The confusion of "they," "there," and "their" is the sort of mistake that all writers are able to catch if they check their work carefully before writing the final draft.

**Wrong:** Soviet defenceman Mikhail Tatarinov is considered to be there enforcer. (*Peterborough Examiner*, Feb. 12, 1987)
**Right:** Soviet defenceman Mikhail Tatarinov is considered to be **their** enforcer.

**Wrong:** There all going to the dance this Saturday.
**Right:** **They're** all going to the dance this Saturday.
**Or:** **They are** all going to the dance this Saturday.

**to/too/two:** "Too" can mean "also" or be used to indicate excess ("too many, too heavy"); "two" is of course the number.

**Wrong:** She seemed to feel that there was to much to do.
**Right:** She seemed to feel that there was **too** much to do.

**vein/vain:** "Veins" run through your body; to be "vain" is to be conceited; an effort that brings no results is in "vain."

**Wrong:** Shakespeare portrays Sir John Oldcastle — or Falstaff, as he is usually known—as vein and irresponsible but immensely amusing and likeable.
**Right:** Shakespeare portrays Sir John Oldcastle — or Falstaff, as

he is usually known—as **vain** and irresponsible but immensely amusing and likeable.

**were/where:** "Were" is of course a past tense form of the verb "to be," while "where" refers to a place.

    **Wrong:**   This is the place were Dante met Beatrice.
    **Right:**   This is the place **where** Dante met Beatrice.

**whose/who's:** "Whose" means "belonging to whom;" "who's" is a contraction of "who is."

    **Wrong:**   Kennedy is not normally remembered as the President who's policies embroiled the US in the Vietnam conflict, but several scholars have suggested that he was as much responsible as was Johnson.
    **Right:**   Kennedy is not normally remembered as the President **whose** policies embroiled the US in the Vietnam conflict, but several scholars have suggested that he was as much responsible as was Johnson.

This list could be much longer, especially if other pairs of homonyms which have variant spellings are considered. Many more are listed in the section on spelling.

A special set of homonyms contains noun-verb pairs which are distinguished by a single sound and spelling difference:

| Noun | Verb |
|---|---|
| advice | advise |
| belief | believe |
| device | devise |
| extent | extend |
| practice | practise |
| prophecy | prophesy |

    **Wrong:**   The wise old man was best remembered for his accurate prophesies; he even prophecied his own death.
    **Right:**   The wise old man was best remembered for his accurate **prophecies**; he even **prophesied** his own death.

    **Wrong:**   The extend to which I can be successful depends on how well you advice me.

**Right:** The **extent** to which I can be successful depends on how well you **advise** me.

# Other Easily Confused Words

Some other words have related spellings and meanings and present similar problems to those of homonyms.

**abstention/abstinence:** An "abstention" is usually a one-off instance of not making a choice or decision, often associated with voting; "abstinence," on the other hand, is the long-term act of not partaking of, most often, alcohol or sex.

**Wrong:** The M.P.'s abstinence was sorely felt as the final vote was lost by a margin of just one.

**Right:** The M.P.'s **abstention** was sorely felt as the final vote was lost by a margin of just one.

**alternately/alternatively:** "Alternately" means "happening in turn," or "first one and then the other"; "alternatively" means "instead of." Be careful as well with the adjectives "alternate" and "alternative."

**Wrong:** An alternate method of arriving at this theoretical value would be to divide the difference between the two prices by the number of warrants.

**Right:** An **alternative** method of arriving at this theoretical value would be to divide the difference between the two prices by the number of warrants.

**Or:** Another method of...

**Wrong:** Professor Beit-Hallahmi seems to have trouble alternatively in reading his own book accurately and in reading my review of it correctly. (Stanley Hoffman, *The New York Review of Books*)

**Right:** Professor Beit-Hallahmi seems to have trouble **alternately** in reading his own book accurately and in reading my review of it correctly.

**anxious/eager:** The adjective "anxious" means "uneasy, nervous, worried;" it should not be used in formal writing to mean "eager."

**Wrong:** He was anxious to help in any way he could.

**Right:** He was **eager** to help in any way he could.

**assure/ensure/insure:** To "assure" someone of something is to tell them with confidence or certainty; to "insure" (or "ensure") that something will happen is to make sure that it does; to "insure" something is to purchase insurance on it so as to protect yourself in case of loss.

> **Wrong:** Our inventory is ensured for $1,000,000.
> **Right:** Our inventory is **insured** for $1,000,000.

**astronomy/astrology:** People who practise both sciences become quite upset when these two are confused. An "astronomer" studies the planets and stars in outer space, while an "astrologer" uses the stars to predict events or compile horoscopes.

> **Wrong:** Her limited knowledge of astronomy told her that she, a Libra, could not possibly be happy with a Taurus.
> **Right:** Her limited knowledge of **astrology** told her that she, a Libra, could not possibly be happy with a Taurus.

**biannual/biennial:** The first means "twice a year," while "biennial" means "once every two years."

> **Wrong:** Some car owners prefer to spread their insurance payments throughout the year instead of making biennial payments in January and July.
> **Right:** Some car owners prefer to spread their insurance payments throughout the year instead of making **biannual** payments in January and July.

**bored, boring: Bored** is the opposite of "interested" and "boring" is the opposite of "interesting ." In other words, one is quite likely to be bored when someone reads out what one has already read in the newspaper, or when one is watching a football game when the score is 38-0, or when one is doing an uninteresting job. To be bored, however, is *not* the same as being sad, or depressed, or irritated, or angry.

> **Wrong:** She was so bored with her husband that she tried to kill him.
> **Right:** She was so **angry** with her husband that she tried to kill him.

**can/may:** In formal writing "can" should be used to refer to ability, "may" to refer to permission.

> **Wrong:** He asked if he could leave the room. (This only makes literal sense if you are talking about an injured person conversing with his doctor.)

> **Right:**   He asked if he **might** leave the room.

**careless/uncaring:** "Careless" means "negligent or thoughtless"; you can be careless about your work, for example, or **careless** about your appearance. Do not use "careless," however, when you want to talk about not caring enough about other people.

> **Wrong:**   He acted in a very careless way towards his mother when she was sick.
>
> **Right:**   He acted in a **heartless** way towards his mother when she was sick.

**childish/childlike:** The first is a term of abuse, the second a term of praise.

> **Wrong:**   Her writing expresses an attractive childish innocence.
>
> **Right:**   Her writing expresses an attractive **childlike** innocence.

**collaborate/corroborate:** To "collaborate" is to work together, whereas to "corroborate" is to give supporting evidence.

> **Wrong:**   He collaborated her claim that the Americans had corroborated with the Nazi colonel Klaus Barbie.
>
> **Right:**   He **corroborated** her claim that the Americans had **collaborated** with the Nazi colonel Klaus Barbie.

**comprise/compose:** The whole "comprises" or includes the various parts; the parts "compose" the whole.

> **Wrong:**   The British government is comprised of far fewer ministries than is the Canadian government.
>
> **Right:**   The British government **comprises** far fewer ministries than does the Canadian government.
>
> **Or:**   The British government **is composed of** far fewer ministries than is the Canadian government.

**conscience/conscious/consciousness:** To be "conscious" is to be awake and aware of what is happening, whereas "conscience" is the part of our mind that tells us it is right to do some things and wrong to do other things (such as steal or murder). "Conscience" and "consciousness" are both nouns; the adjectives are "conscientious" (aware of what is right and wrong) and "conscious" (aware).

> **Wrong:**   She was tempted to steal the chocolate bar, but her **conscious** told her not to.
>
> **Right:**   She was tempted to steal the chocolate bar, but her "conscience" told her not to.

**contagious/infectious:** Both are used when referring to the communication of disease. "Contagious" requires touch, while **infectious** diseases can be spread through being in close proximity to the disease.

> **Wrong:** The police wore masks to interview the victim because his disease was highly contagious.
> **Right:** The police wore masks to interview the victim because his disease was highly **infectious**.

**contemptuous/contemptible:** We are "contemptuous" of anyone or anything we find "contemptible."

> **Wrong:** The judge called the delinquent's behavior utterly contemptuous.
> **Right:** The judge called the delinquent's behavior utterly **contemptible**.

**continual/continuous:** If something is "continuous" it never stops; something "continual" is frequently repeated but not unceasing. The same distinction holds for the adverbs "continually" and "continuously."

> **Wrong:** He has been phoning me continuously for the past two weeks. (Surely he stopped for a bite to eat or a short nap.)
> **Right:** He has been phoning me **continually** for the past two weeks.

**credible/credulous:** Someone "credulous" (believing) is likely to believe anything, even if it is not "credible" (believable).

> **Wrong:** "Maybe I'm too credible," she said. "I believe everything my husband tells me."
> **Right:** "Maybe I'm too **credulous**," she said. "I believe everything my husband tells me."

**deduce/deduct:** "Deduction" is the noun stemming from both these verbs, which is perhaps why they are sometimes confused. To "deduce" is to draw a conclusion, whereas to "deduct" is to subtract.

> **Wrong:** Sherlock Holmes deducted that Moriarty had committed the crime.
> **Right:** Sherlock Holmes **deduced** that Moriarty had committed the crime.

**degradation/decline:** "Degradation" carries the connotation of shame and disgrace; certain military spokespeople have been making every attempt to corrupt it. To "degrade" something is not to reduce it, or downgrade it, or destroy it.

**Wrong:** Among those units in which women played a combat role there was no degradation in operational effectiveness. (CBC news, April 30, 1987)

**Right:** Among those units in which women played a combat role there was no **decline** in operational effectiveness.

**Or:** ...there was no **reduction** in operational effectiveness.

**Wrong:** According to US authorities, the Iraqi threat has now been significantly **degraded**. (Global news, January 24, 1991)

**Right:** According to US authorities, the Iraqi threat has now been significantly **reduced**.

**definite/definitive:** If something is "definite" then there is no uncertainty about it; a "definitive" version of something fixes it in its final or permanent form—just as a dictionary definition attempts to fix the meaning of a word. Often a sentence is better with neither of these words.

**Wrong:** Glenn Gould's recording of Bach's *Brandenburg Concertos* is often thought of as the definite modern version.

**Right:** Glenn Gould's recording of Bach's *Brandenburg Concertos* is often thought of as the **definitive** modern version.

**Wrong:** Once we have completed our caucus discussion I will be making a very definitive statement.

**Right:** Once we have completed our caucus discussion I will be making a statement.

**Or:** Once we have completed our caucus discussion I will have something **definite** to say.

**deny/refute:** To "deny" something is to assert that it is not true; to "refute" it is to prove conclusively that it is not true.

**Wrong:** He was unable to deny the allegations. (This could only be true if, for example, he were in a coma.)

**Right:** He was unable to **refute** the allegations.

**deprecate/depreciate:** To "deprecate" something is to suggest that it is not valuable or worthy of praise; something that "depreciates" loses its value.

**Wrong:** Robert Stanfield is a very self-depreciating man.

**Right:** Robert Stanfield is a very self-**deprecating** man.

**disinterested/uninterested:** A "disinterested" person is unbiased; uninfluenced by self-interest, especially of a monetary sort. It is thus quite possible for a person who is entirely "disinterested" in a particular matter to be completely fascinated by it. If one is "uninterested" in something, on the other hand, one is bored by it.

> **Wrong:** He was so disinterested in the game that he left after the fifth inning with the score at 2-2.
> **Right:** He was so **uninterested** in the game that he left after the fifth inning with the score at 2-2.

> **Wrong:** It was vintage Reagan: stumbling over his text, unsure of his facts, disinterested in the topic at hand. (*The Toronto Star*, Nov. 15, 1987)
> **Right:** It was vintage Reagan: stumbling over his text, unsure of his facts, **uninterested** in the topic at hand.

**distinct/distinctive:** "Distinct" means "able to be seen or perceived clearly; easily distinguishable from those around it." **Distinctive** means "unusual; not commonly found." There is a similar contrast between the adverbs "distinctly" and "distinctively," and the nouns "distinction" and "distinctiveness."

> **Wrong:** I distinctively heard the sound of a car engine.
> **Right:** I **distinctly** heard the sound of a car engine.

**effective/efficacious/effectual/efficient:** "Effective, efficacious and effectual" all mean sufficient to produce the desired effect. "Efficacious," however, applies only to things: a person cannot be efficacious. "Effectual" was once applied only to actions, but is now sometimes applied to people as well. "Effective" can apply to actions or people, and has an added connotation: producing results with little waste of money or effort. Thus a promotional campaign to persuade people to buy a product by giving away free samples to every man, woman, and child in the country might be "effective," but it would certainly not be "efficient"; a good deal of waste would be involved. The same difference applies to the nouns "effectiveness" and "efficiency." ("Efficacy" is a rather pretentious noun that is usually best avoided.)

> **Wrong:** The Board wants to increase the efficacy of the machinery we use.
> **Right:** The Board wants to increase the **efficiency** of the machinery we use.

> **Poor:** It would not be efficacious to launch a direct mail campaign with a product of this sort.
> **Better:** It would not be **effective** to launch a direct mail campaign with a product of this sort.

**elemental/elementary:** "Elemental" refers to the basic elements (fire, water, air, and earth), while "elementary" is an adjective which means "basic."

> **Wrong:** My friends and I are taking a course in elemental German.
> **Right:** My friends and I are taking a course in **elementary** German.

**enervate/invigorate**: Because of the similarity in sound between "enervate" and "energy," it is often thought to mean "make more energetic." In fact it means just the opposite—"to lessen the strength of." If something makes you more energetic it invigorates you.

> **Wrong:** She found the fresh air quite enervating; I haven't seen her so lively in months.
> **Right:** She found the fresh air quite **invigorating**; I haven't seen her so lively in months.

**epithet/epigraph/epitaph/epigram:** four words often confused. Here are their meanings:

> **Epithet** an adjective or short phrase describing someone (*"The Golden Brett*, the epithet often used to describe Brett Hull, involves an allusion to the nickname of his famous father.")
>
> **Epigraph** an inscription, especially one placed upon a building, tomb, or statue to indicate its name or purpose
>
> **Epitaph** words describing a dead person, often the words inscribed on the tomb
>
> **Epigram** a short, witty or pointed saying
>
> **wrong** His epigram will read, "A good man lies here."
> **Right:** His **epitaph** will read, "A good man lies here."

**equal/equitable/equable:** Things that are "equal" have the same value. Arrangements that are "equitable" are fair and just. An "equable" person is one who is moderate and even-tempered.

> **Wrong:** The distribution of Commons and Senate seats is an equable one; in almost every case the percentage of combined seats allocated to a province closely approximates the percentage of the Canadian population made up by its inhabitants.
> **right** The distribution of Commons and Senate seats is an **equitable** one; in almost every case the percentage of

combined seats allocated to a province closely
approximates the percentage of the Canadian population
made up by its inhabitants.

**explicit/implicit:** If something is "explicit" it is "unfolded"—stated in precise terms, not merely suggested or implied. Something that is "implicit" is "folded in"—not stated overtly. By extension "implicit" has also come to mean "complete" or "absolute" in expressions such as "implicit trust" (i.e., trust so complete that it does not have to be put into words).

> **Wrong:** I told you **implicitly** to have the report on my desk first thing this morning.
>
> **Right:** I told you **explicitly** to have the report on my desk first thing in the morning.

**flout/flaunt:** To "flout" is to disobey or show disrespect for; to "flaunt" is to display very openly.

> **Wrong:** Aggressive policing seems to have increased the number of people flaunting the law. (*Peterborough This Week*, May 17, 1992)
>
> **Right:** Aggressive policing seems to have increased the number of people **flouting** the law.

**fortunate/fortuitous:** "Fortunate" means lucky; "fortuitous" means happening by chance.

> **Wrong:** This combination of circumstances is not a fortuitous one for our company; we shall have to expect reduced sales in the coming year.
>
> **Right:** This combination of circumstances is not a **fortunate** one for our company; we shall have to expect reduced sales in the coming year.

**founder/flounder:** As a verb, "founder" means "to get into difficulty; to stumble or fall, to sink" (when speaking of a ship), or "to fail" (when speaking of a plan). To "flounder" is "to move clumsily or with difficulty," or "to become confused" in an effort to do something.

> **Wrong:** He foundered about in a hopeless attempt to solve the problem.
>
> **Right:** He **floundered** about in a hopeless attempt to solve the problem.

**human/humane:** Until the eighteenth century there was no distinction made between the two in either meaning or pronunciation; they were simply alternative ways of spelling the same word. In recent centuries "humane" has come to be used to refer exclusively to the more attractive human qualities—kindness, compassion and so forth.

> **Wrong:** Their group is campaigning for the human treatment of animals.
> **Right:** Their group is campaigning for the **humane** treatment of animals.

**imply/infer:** To "imply" something is to suggest it without stating it directly; the other person will have to **infer** your meaning. It may be a comfort to the many who have confused the two to know that the mistake goes back at least as far as Milton:

> **Wrong:** Great or Bright infers not Excellence. (*Paradise Lost* viii, 91)
> **Right:** Great or Bright **implies** not Excellence. (The fact that a thing is great or bright does not imply that it is also excellent.)

> **Wrong:** I implied from his tone that he disliked our plan.
> **Right:** I **inferred** from his tone that he disliked our plan.

**incredible/incredulous:** These are not synonyms—"incredible" means "unbelievable," while "incredulous" means "unbelieving."

> **Wrong:** The whole story was so incredulous—we just could not believe it.
> **Right:** The whole story was so **incredible**—we just could not believe it (therefore, we were **incredulous**).

**insist/persist:** To "insist" (that something be done, *or* on doing something) is to express yourself very forcefully. To "persist" in doing something is to keep on doing it, usually despite some difficulty or opposition.

> **Wrong:** Even after he had been convicted of the crime, he persisted that he was innocent.
> **Right:** Even after he had been convicted of the crime, he **insisted** that he was innocent.

**instinctive/instinctual:** There is no difference in meaning; it is thus better to stay with the older (and more pleasant sounding) "instinctive."

> **Poor:** Biologists disagree as to what constitutes instinctual behavior.
> **Better:** Biologists disagree as to what constitutes **instinctive** behavior

**judicial/judicious:** "Judicial" means "having to do with law courts and the administration of justice." "Judicious" means "having good judgment."

> **Wrong:** He made one or two judicial comments about the quality of the production.
>
> **Right:** He made one or two **judicious** comments about the quality of the production.

**later/latter:** "Later" means "afterwards in time", whereas the "latter" is the last mentioned (of two things).

> **Wrong:** I looked up the battle of Stalingrad in both the *World Book* and the *Encyclopaedia Britannica*. The later provided much more information.
>
> **Right:** I looked up the battle of Stalingrad in both the *World Book* and the *Encyclopaedia Britannica*. The **latter** provided much more information.

**laudable/laudatory:** "Laudable" means "worthy of praise;" **laudatory** means "expressing praise."

> **Wrong:** His efforts to combat poverty are very **laudatory**.
>
> **Right:** His efforts to combat poverty are very **laudable**.

**libel/slander:** "Libel" is written (and published); "slander" is oral.

> **Wrong:** He was careful in his speech to avoid making any libellous remarks.
>
> **Right:** He was careful in his speech to avoid making any **slanderous** remarks.

**masterful/masterly:** To do something in a "masterly" way means to do it very skilfully, while "masterful" indicates performing an action in an almost oppressive way.

> **Wrong:** His expertise allowed him to close the wound in a masterful way.
>
> **Right:** His expertise allowed him to close the wound in a **masterly** way.

**meantime/meanwhile:** "Meantime" is a noun, used most frequently in the phrase "in the meantime." "Meanwhile" is an adverb.

> **wrong** The Germans were preparing for an attack near Calais. Meantime, the Allies were readying themselves for the invasion of Normandy.

**right**   The Germans were preparing for an attack near Calais. **Meanwhile**, the Allies were readying themselves for the invasion of Normandy.

**mitigate/militate:** To "mitigate" something is to make it less harsh or severe; thus "mitigating" circumstances are those that make a criminal offence less serious. To "militate" against something is to act as a strong influence against it.

**Wrong:**   The natural history orientation of early anthropology also mitigated against studies of change. (Bruce G. Trigger in *Natives and Newcomers*)

**Right:**   The natural history orientation of early anthropology also **militated** against studies of change.

**partake/participate:** "Partake" refers to things (especially food and drink), "participate" to activities.

**Wrong:**   The Governor General made a brief appearance, but did not partake in the festivities.

**Right:**   The Governor General made a brief appearance, but did not **participate** in the festivities.

**per cent/percentage:** If you use "per cent," you must give the number. Otherwise, use "percentage."

**Wrong:**   The per cent of people surveyed who reported any change of opinion was very small.

**Right:**   The **percentage** of people surveyed who reported any change of opinion was very small.

**Or:**   Only six **per cent** of the people surveyed reported any change of opinion.

Note: "Percentage" is always one word; authorities differ as to whether "per cent" should always be written as as two words, or whether it also may be written as one word.

**persecute/prosecute:** To "persecute" someone is to treat them in a harsh and unfair manner, especially because of their political or religious beliefs. To "prosecute" someone is to take legal action against them in the belief that they have committed a crime.

**Wrong:**   Catholics began to be prosecuted in England in the sixteenth century.

**Right:**   Catholics began to be **persecuted** in England in the sixteenth century.

**practical/practicable:** "Practical" means "suitable for use," or "involving activity rather than theory." "Practicable" means "able to be done." Changing the railway system back to steam locomotives would be "practicable" but extremely "impractical." In most cases "practical" is the word the writer wants; excessive use of "practicable" will make writing sound pretentious rather than important.

> **Wrong:** We do not feel that the construction of a new facility would be practicable at this time.
>
> **Right:** It would not be **practical** to construct a new facility now.

**proposition/proposal:** The only formally correct meaning of "proposition" is a statement that expresses an idea, as in "This country is dedicated to the proposition that all men are created equal." It is better not to use it to mean "proposal."

> **Poor:** The department has put forward a proposition for increasing sales.
>
> **Better:** The department has put forward a **proposal** for increasing sales.

**quote/quotation:** "Quote" is the verb, "quotation" the noun.

> **Wrong:** The following quote shows just how determined Trudeau was to patriate the Constitution.
>
> **Right:** The following **quotation** shows just how determined Trudeau was to patriate the Constitution.

**raise/rise:** "Raise" means "to lift"; "rise" means "to come up."

> **Wrong:** They rose the curtain at 8 o'clock.
>
> **Right:** They **raised** the curtain at 8 o'clock.
>
> **Or:** The curtain **rose** at 8 o'clock.

**real/genuine:** The basic meaning of "real" is "existing"; the opposite of "fake" or "forged" is "genuine."

> **Poor:** The buyer had thought the painting was a Cézanne, but he soon discovered it was not real.
>
> **Better:** The buyer had thought the painting was a Cézanne, but he soon discovered it was not **genuine**.

**respectively/respectfully:** "Respectively" means "in the order mentioned"; "respectfully" means "done with respect."

> **Wrong:** San Diego, Chicago, and Miami were, respectfully, the three best teams in the NFL last season.

**Right:** San Diego, Chicago, and Miami were, **respectively**, the three best teams in the NFL last season.

**revenge/avenge:** The former is most often used as a noun, as in to "take revenge," while the latter is the more common verb.

**Poor:** Orestes aimed to revenge the death of his father Agamemnon.
**Better:** Orestes aimed to **avenge** the death of his father Agamemnon.

**sensory/sensuous/sensual:** Advertising and pornography have dulled the distinction among these three adjectives. The meanings of "sensory" and "sensuous" are similar—"sensual" is the sexy one:

**Sensory** having to do with the senses

**Sensuous** having to do with the senses, or appealing to the senses

**Sensual** offering physical pleasure, especially of a sexual sort

**Wrong:** Boswell suggested they go to a house of ill repute, but Johnson had no desire for sensuous pleasures.
**Right:** Boswell suggested they go to a house of ill repute, but Johnson had no desire for **sensual** pleasures.

**set/sit:** "Set" means "to place something somewhere."

**Wrong:** I could remember everything, but I had difficulty sitting it down on paper.
**Right:** I could remember everything, but I had difficulty **setting** it down on paper.

**Wrong:** He asked me to set down on the couch.
**Right:** He asked me to **sit** down on the couch.

**simple/simplistic:** "Simplistic" is a derogatory word meaning "too simple" or "excessively simplified".

**Wrong:** The questions were so simplistic that I was able to answer all but one correctly.
**Right:** The questions were so **simple** that I was able to answer all but one correctly.

**specially/especially:** "Specially" means "for a particular purpose" ("These utensils are specially designed for left-handed people.") "Especially" means "particularly" or "more than in other cases."

> **Wrong:** The entire system pleased her, but she was was specially happy to see that the computer program had been especially created for small business users.
>
> **Right:** The entire system pleased her, but she was **especially** happy to see that the computer program had been **specially** created for small business users.

**stimulant/stimulus:** "Stimulus" (plural "stimuli") is the more general word for anything that produces a reaction; "stimulant" normally refers to a drink or drug that has a "stimulating" effect.

> **Wrong:** The shocks were intended to act as stimulants to the rats that we used as subjects for the experiment.
>
> **Right:** The shocks were intended to act as **stimuli** to the rats that we used as subjects for the experiment.

**supposed to/should:** These two are very similar in meaning, and may often be used interchangeably; if a person is "supposed to" do something, then that is what she "should" do. In the <u>past</u> tense, however, the question of when and when not to use "supposed to" is quite tricky. You <u>may</u> use it when you are clearly talking about a <u>fixed plan</u> that has not been carried out (e.g., "He was supposed to arrive before two o'clock, but he is still not here"). You <u>should not</u> use it to apply to any action that you think was wrong, or you feel should not have been carried out. The safe solution to this problem is to always use "should" instead of "supposed to."

> **Wrong:** What she said was impolite, but he was not supposed to hit her for saying it.
>
> **Right:** What she said was impolite, but he **should not** have hit her for saying it.

> **Wrong:** The South African government was not supposed to keep Nelson Mandela in jail for so many years.
>
> **Right:** The South African government should not have kept Nelson Mandela in jail for so many years.

**sympathy/empathy/apathy:** All three words are related: "sympathy" means an expression of feelings which console someone in their grief; "empathy" means an understanding of someone's feelings as if they were your own. It can also mean a deep understanding of a work of art. "Apathy," on the other hand, indicates a lack of emotional feeling.

> **Wrong:** The mourners came to the funeral to show the widow

their deepest apathy.

**Right:** The mourners came to the funeral to show the widow their deepest **sympathy**.

**But:** The onlookers felt great **empathy** for the mourners as they left the funeral in slow procession.

**tack/tact:** "Tack" is a sailing term; a different tack means "a different direction relative to the wind." "Tact" is skill in saying or doing the right or polite thing.

**Wrong:** We will have to exercise all our tack in the coming negotiations.

**Right:** We will have to exercise all our **tact** in the coming negotiations.

**thankful/grateful:** We are "thankful" that something has happened, and "grateful" for something we have received.

**Wrong:** I am very thankful for the kind thoughts expressed in your letter.

**Right:** I am very **grateful** for the kind thoughts expressed in your letter.

**tiring/tiresome:** Something that is "tiring" makes you feel tired, though you may have enjoyed it very much. Something that is "tiresome" is tedious and unpleasant.

**Wrong:** Although it is tiresome for him, my father likes to play tennis at least twice a week.

**Right:** Although it is **tiring** for him, my father likes to play tennis at least twice a week.

**unexceptional/unexceptionable:** "Unexceptional" means ordinary, not an exception; "unexceptionable" means you do not object (or take exception) to the thing or person in question.

**Wrong:** One way Reagan pays for this is in the confusion and controversy that surround the unexceptional White House plan to reflag 11 Kuwaiti tankers with the Stars and Stripes. It is a modest proposal that in itself should not cause the handwringing now being observed on Capitol Hill. (*The Washington Post*, July 20 1987) (The plan to reflag the tankers clearly <u>was</u> an exception; the U.S. had not done anything similar for years. What the writer means to say is that the plan is **unexceptionable**—that no one should have any objection to it.)

**Right:** One way Reagan pays for this is in the confusion and controversy that surround the **unexceptionable** White House plan to reflag 11 Kuwaiti tankers with the Stars and Stripes. It is a modest proposal that in itself should not cause the handwringing now being observed on Capitol Hill.

**verbal/oral:** "Oral" means "spoken rather than written," whereas **verbal** means "having to do with words." A person who is unable to speak may have a high level of "verbal" skill.

**Wrong:** I can write well enough, but I have difficulty in expressing ideas verbally.

**Right:** I can write well enough, but I have difficulty in expressing ideas **orally**.

# Confusing Adjectives

Some adjectives can take an -al ending to form a different adjective. Frequently, this new adjective has a distinct meaning from the one without the suffix, and the two cannot be used interchangeably. At other times, however, the words are practically synonymous. Take care not to create -al adjectives which do not exist—it is often overkill to attempt to form an -al adjective when the simple one will do.

**-al adjective with distinct meanings**

**classic/classical:** "Classic" means something that is of such great quality that it is likely to endure; it can also be used when referring to an ideal example of something, as in a classic line from an old film. "Classical," however, refers to ancient Greece and Rome, and also to music which dates from the Classical period (c. 1750-1830); without capitalization, it also refers to any music which is not jazz, popular, rock, or country and which is usually played by orchestras or sung by trained choral or operatic performers.

**Wrong:** Sophocles was one of the greatest classic authors; his plays are classical.

**Right:** Sophocles was one of the greatest **classical** authors; his plays are considered to be **classics**.

**comic/comical:** "Comic" is often restricted to certain compounds, as in "comic opera" or "comic book." It is also used when something is intentionally comical. On the other hand, "comical" is often used when the speaker wishes to show that something was unintentionally (or unfortunately) funny.

> **Wrong:** The whole debate degenerated into a farce—it was really comic.
>
> **Right:** The whole debate degenerated into a farce — it was really **comical**.

**economic/economical:** "Economic" means pertaining to economics, or sufficient to allow a reasonable return for the amount of money or effort put in. "Economical" is a word applied to people, which means thrifty. The difference applies as well to "uneconomic" and "uneconomical."

> **Wrong:** The government's policies, especially their economical ones, are widely criticized.
>
> **Right:** The government's policies, especially their **economic** ones, are widely criticized.

**historic/historical:** "Historic" means "of sufficient importance that it is likely to become famous in history"; "historical" means "having to do with history" (historical research, historical scholarship, etc.).

> **Wrong:** We are gathered here for an historical occasion—the opening of the city's first sewage treatment plant.
>
> **Right:** We are gathered here for an **historic** occasion—the opening of the city's first sewage treatment plant.

# Interchangeable Adjectives

These adjectives which end in -al are much more common than their basic equivalents, perhaps because the adjective without -al can also be a noun form.

> **fanatic:** fanatical
>
> **hysteric:** hysterical
>
> **ironic:** ironical
>
> **mystic:** mystical

## Some -al adjectives which do not exist

> **Wrong:** The prisoner was shot as he made a frantical attempt to scale the fence.
>
> **Right:** The prisoner was shot as he made a **frantic** attempt to scale the fence.

> **Wrong:** This paper will show the tragical flaw in the character of
> Oedipus that led him to his pathetical end.
> **Right:** This paper will show the **tragic** flaw in the character of
> Oedipus that led him to his **pathetic** end.

# Problems with Usage

**according to:** This expression normally is used only when one is referring to a
person or to a group of people (e.g., "According to his lawyer, the accused was
nowhere near the scene when the crime was committed"; "According to Shakespeare, Richard III was an evil king").

> **Wrong:** According to geography, Zaire is larger than all of
> Western Europe.
> **Right:** **As** we learn in geography, Zaire is larger than all of
> Western Europe.

> **Wrong:** According to the story of *Cry the Beloved Country*, Stephen
> Kumalo has a quick temper.
> **Right:** The events of the story show that Stephen Kumalo has a
> quick temper.

**amount:** This word should only be used with things that are uncountable (sugar,
rice, etc.).

> **Wrong:** A large amount of books were stolen from the library last
> night.
> **Right:** A large **number** of books were stolen from the library
> last night.

**be/have:** A number of languages have expressions that use the verb "have"
where English must use the verb "be." Common expressions include those indicating feelings, like hunger, thirst, pain, anger, etc., and expressions of age.

> **Wrong:** Let's eat—I have hungry or I have hunger.
> **Right:** Let's eat—I'm hungry.

> **Wrong:** You'll never believe how old that new teacher is—he has
> only 24.
> **Right:** You'll never believe how old that new teacher is—he's
> only 24.

**both:** The expressions "both alike," "both equal," and "both together" involve
repetition.

**Poor:** Macdonald and Cartier both arrived together at about eight o'clock.

**Better:** Macdonald and Cartier arrived together at about eight o'clock.

**change:** You make a "change" (not *do* a change).

**Wrong:** The manager did several changes to the roster before the match with the Soviet Union.

**Right:** The manager **made** several changes to the roster before the match with the Soviet Union.

**comment:** We make comments (not say or do them).

**Wrong:** Anyone who wishes to say any comments will have a chance to speak after the lecture.

**Right:** Anyone who wishes to **make** any comments will have a chance to speak after the lecture.

**convince:** You "convince" people that they should do something, or **persuade** them to do it.

**Wrong:** Reagan's advisers convinced him to approve the arms for hostages deal with Iran.

**Right:** Reagan's advisers **persuaded** him to approve the arms for hostages deal with Iran.

**for:** One use of this preposition is to show purpose. Normally, however, "for" can only be used in this way when the purpose can be expressed in one word (e.g., "for safety," "for security"). It is *not* usually correct to try to express purpose by combining "for" with a pronoun and an infinitive: expressions such as "for him to be happy," "for us to arrive safely" are awkward and should be avoided. Instead, one can express purpose either by beginning with an infinitive (e.g., "in order to make life easier, in order to increase yield per hectare"), or by using "so that" (e.g., "so that life will be made easier," "so that yield per hectare will be increased").

**Wrong:** Please speak slowly for me to understand what you say.

**Right:** Please speak slowly **so that I can** understand what you say.

**Wrong:** The team must work hard for it to have a chance at the Grey Cup.

**Right:** The team must work hard **if it is** to have a chance at the Grey Cup.

**forget:** "To forget" something is to fail to remember it, <u>not</u> to leave it some-where.

> **Wrong:** I forgot my textbook at home.
> **Right:** I **left** my textbook at home.
> **Or:** I **forgot** to bring my textbook from home.

**how/what:** One may talk about "how" something (or someone) *is*, or "what" something (or someone) is like, but <u>not</u> "how" they are like.

> **Wrong:** Tell me how it looks like from where you are.
> **Right:** Tell me how it looks from where you are.
> **Or:** Tell me what it looks like from where you are.

> **Wrong:** I do not know how the roads are like between St. John's and Cornerbrook.
> **Right:** I do not know what the roads are like between St. John's and Cornerbrook.
> **Or:** I do not know how the roads are between St. John's and Cornerbrook.

**increase:** Numbers can be "increased" or "decreased," as can such things as production and population (nouns which refer to certain types of numbers or quantities). Things such as houses, however, or books (nouns which do not refer to numbers or quantities) cannot be "increased"; only the <u>number</u> of houses, books etc. can be "increased" or "decreased," raised or lowered.

> **Wrong:** The government has greatly increased low-rent houses in the suburbs of Toronto.
> **Right:** The government has greatly **increased the number of** low-rent houses in the suburbs of Toronto.

**information:** One <u>gives</u> "information" (*not* <u>tells it</u>).

> **Wrong:** He told me all the information I wanted about how to apply.
> **Right:** He **gave** me all the **information** I wanted about how to apply.

**investigation:** We <u>make</u>, <u>carry out</u>, or <u>hold</u> an "investigation" (not <u>do</u> one).

> **Wrong:** The manager did a thorough investigation into the disappearance of funds from his department.
> **Right:** The manager **made** a thorough investigation into the disappearance of funds from his department.

**journey:** You <u>make</u> a "journey" (not <u>do</u> one).

> **Wrong:**  If we do not stop along the way, we can do the journey in an hour.
>
> **Right:**  If we do not stop along the way, we can **make** the **journey** in an hour.

**know/can:** Do not confuse these two verbs when expressing ability to do something because of skill or knowledge. "Can" means "be able," i.e. indicating physical capability or being permitted, as in "I cannot come out tonight." It can also mean "be able" because of an acquired level of knowledge or expertise that allows you to perform or act in an informed way, as in "Can you play the piano?" "Know," on the other hand, must be accompanied by "how to" if a meaning similar to "can" is sought.

> **Wrong:**  She must be very clever because she "knows" to play the piano.
>
> **Right:**  She must be very clever because she **can** play the piano.
>
> **Or:**  She must be very clever because she **knows how to** play the piano.

"Know to" means to "have the sense to" do something, as in "When walking alone, I know to be on the lookout for strangers."

Note that when an adverb is used, "can" is preferable to "know how to."

> **Poor:**  He'll be in the Olympics next time because he knows how to ski really well.
>
> **Better:**  He'll be in the Olympics next time because he **can** ski really well.

**less/fewer:** When something can be counted (e.g., people, books, trees), use "fewer." Use "less" only with <u>uncountable</u> nouns (e.g., *sugar, meat, equipment*).

> **Wrong:**  There are less people here than there were last week.
>
> **Right:**  There are **fewer** people here than there were last week.

> **Wrong:**  There are less steps and that means there is more room for error. (*Financial Post*, Nov. 20, 1989)
>
> **Right:**  There are **fewer** steps and that means there is more room for error.

**many/much:** "Many" is used for countable nouns like "people" and "desks." "Much," on the other hand, can only be used with uncountable nouns like "trouble" or "sugar." One way to check: if you cannot replace "many" with a number like "two," you should use "much" instead.

**Wrong:** There were much people shopping on Christmas Eve.
**Right:** There were **many** people shopping on Christmas Eve.

**mistake:** "Mistakes" are <u>made</u> (not <u>done</u>).

**Wrong:** He did seven mistakes in that short spelling exercise.
**Right:** He **made** seven **mistakes** in that short spelling exercise.

**momentarily:** "Momentarily" means "lasting only a moment" ("He was momentarily confused"). Common usage also allows the word to mean "in a moment" or "soon;" in formal writing it is best to avoid this use.

**Poor:** Ms. Billings has informed me that she will join us momentarily.
**Better:** Ms. Billings told me that she will join us **soon**.

**opposed:** You are "opposed" <u>to</u> something or someone (not <u>with</u> or <u>against</u>).

**Wrong:** Charles Darwin was opposed against the literal interpretation of the story of Creation, as found in *Genesis*.
**Right:** Charles Darwin was **opposed to** the literal interpretation of the story of Creation, as found in *Genesis*.

**other:** if one uses the words <u>the</u> "other" it suggests that the thing or person one is about to mention is the <u>only</u> "other" one is going to write about. If there are several others to be mentioned, **another** is the word to choose.

**Wrong:** One reason why Germany lost the Second World War was that she underestimated the importance of keeping the United States out of the conflict. The other reason was that her intelligence network was inferior to that of the Allies. Moreover, Hitler's decision to invade Russia was a disastrous mistake.

(Here the use of the "other" in the second sentence leads the reader to believe this is the <u>only</u> other reason. When a third reason is mentioned in the next sentence, the reader is taken by surprise.)

**Right:** One reason why Germany lost the Second World War was that she underestimated the importance of keeping the United States out of the conflict. **Another** reason was that her intelligence network was inferior to that of the Allies. Moreover, Hitler's decision to invade Russia was a disastrous mistake.

**persuade:** To "persuade" someone of something is to make them believe that it is true. To persuade them to do something is to lead them, through what one says, to do the desired thing. If one does not succeed in making them believe or do what one wants, then one has not persuaded or convinced them, but only <u>tried</u> to persuade them.

> **Wrong:** After all Portia's persuasion Shylock still refuses to change his mind.
>
> **Right:** After all Portia's attempts **to persuade him**, Shylock still refuses to change his mind.

**presently:** This is the subject of much disagreement among grammarians: should presently be restricted to its original meaning of "soon," or should common usage of the word to mean "now" be allowed to spread unopposed? Traditionalists argue that the acceptance of both meanings encourages ambiguity, but in fact the verb tense usually makes clear whether the speaker means "soon" or "now" ("I will be there presently"; "I am presently working on a large project", etc.). Perhaps the best solution is to avoid the rather pompous "presently" altogether, and stick to those fine Anglo-Saxon words "soon" and "now."

> **Poor:** I am seeing Mr. Jones presently.
>
> **Better:** I am seeing Mr. Jones **now**.
>
> **Or:** I will be seeing Mr. Jones **soon**.

**since/for:** Both these words can be used to indicate length (or duration) of time, but they are used in slightly different ways. "Since" is used to mention the <u>point</u> at which a period of time began ("since 6 o'clock", "since 1980", "since last Christmas", etc.). "For" is used to mention the <u>amount</u> of time that has passed ("for two years," "for six months," "for centuries," etc.).

> **Wrong:** She has been staying with us since three weeks.
>
> **Right:** She has been staying with us **for** three weeks.
>
> **Or:** She has been staying with us **since** three weeks <u>ago</u>.

**so:** When used to show degree or extent, "so" is normally used with "that": "so big that...," "so hungry that..." , etc. "So" should not be used as an intensifier in the way that "very" is used.

> **Wrong:** When she stepped out of the church she looked so beautiful.
>
> **Right:** When she stepped out of the church she looked **very** beautiful.
>
> **Or:** When she stepped out of the church she looked **so** beautiful that it was hard to believe she had once been thought of as plain.

**somehow:** "Somehow" means "by some method" ("Somehow I must repair my car so that I can arrive in time for my appointment"). It does not mean "in some ways, to some extent," or "somewhat".

> **Wrong:** His brother is somehow mentally disturbed.
> **Right:** His brother is mentally disturbed **in some way**.
> **Or:** His brother is **somewhat** disturbed mentally.

**unique/universal/perfect/complete/correct:** None of these can be a matter of degree. Something is either unique or not unique, perfect or imperfect, and so on.

> **Wrong:** Fathers may have a relatively unique contribution to make to family functioning and the development of the child.
> **Right:** Fathers may have a **unique** contribution to make to family functioning and the development of the child.

**valid/true/accurate:** An "accurate" statement is one that is factually correct. A combination of "accurate" facts may not always give a "true" picture, however. For example, the statement that former Canadian Prime Minister Mackenzie King often visited prostitutes is entirely "accurate," but gives a false impression; in fact King visited prostitutes to try to convince them of the error of their ways, not to use their services. "Valid" has become so overused and fuzzy in its meaning that it is best avoided. Properly used it can mean "legally acceptable," or "sound in reasoning." Usually it is best to use "accurate" or "true," or "well-founded."

> **Poor:** Churchill's fear that the Nazis would become a threat to the rest of Europe turned out to be valid.
> **Better:** Churchill's fear that the Nazis would become a threat to the rest of Europe turned out to be **well-founded**.

# Affixes

Affixes are particles which are fixed on to a word, either at the beginning (prefixes) or at the end (suffixes). They are extremely useful, since they can alter the meaning of a root verb, noun, or adjective in a number of different ways while still retaining some sense of the original meaning. There is great flexibility in being able to add short affixes to words to change their meaning or function within a sentence. However, as might be expected, certain problems can arise when identifying and using affixes.

## A checklist of common affixes

| Affix | Meaning | Examples |
|---|---|---|

### Prefixes

| Affix | Meaning | Examples |
|---|---|---|
| ab- | "away from" | abduct, aberrant |
| ante- | "before" | antenatal, antecedent |
| anti- | "against"/"opposed" | antiperspirant, antithesis |
| a- | "without" | asexual, apathetic |
| bi- | "two" | bicycle, biped |
| co- | "with" | cooperate, coexist |
| de- | reverses action | decompose, degenerate |
| extra- | "outside of" | extramural, extraordinary |
| ex- | "out of" | exhale, expectorate |
| hyper- | "over"/"in excess" | hyperactive, hyperbole |
| inter- | "between"/"among" | international, interrelate |
| intra- | "within" | intramural, intravenous |
| in- | (a) "not" | incomplete, inactive |
| | (b) "into" | inhale, influx |
| multi- | "many" | multicoloured, multiply |
| post- | "after" | post-mortem, postnatal |
| pre- | "before" | preamble, preview |
| pro- | (a) "in front of" | proboscis |
| | (b) "in place of" | pronoun |
| | (c) "before" | prospectus |
| re- | "again" | reiterate, recurring |
| sub- | "below" | submarine, substandard |
| super- | above" | supersonic, supervise |
| ultra- | "above and beyond" | ultraviolet, ultrasonic |
| un- | "not" | unhealthy, unpopular |

### Suffixes

| Affix | Meaning | Examples |
|---|---|---|
| -al | forms adjective | phenomenal, inspirational |
| -ful | "full of" | beautiful, thankful |
| -ic | forms adjective | patriotic, idiotic |
| -ing | forms present participle | reading, motivating |
| -ion | forms noun from verb | interrogation, domination |
| -ish | "not exactly"/"like" | reddish, biggish |
| -ism | forms noun | patriotism, feminism |
| -ity | forms noun from adjective | spontaneity, purity |
| -less | "without" | hopeless, jobless |

| | | |
|---|---|---|
| **-ly** | "in this way" | happily, mercifully |
| **-ness** | forms noun from adjective | happiness, hopelessness |
| **-ship** | forms noun from adjective | hardship, |

One of the first dangers surrounding affixes is using the wrong affix to create another form of a word. For example, the list above shows a number of different ways of forming nouns from adjectives. The method of deriving a noun from an adjective should be learned in each case. An educated guess by analogy with another form (or even a wild guess) can sometimes work, but it can frequently yield a word which does not exist.

**Wrong:** What made it even better was the spontaneousness of the whole thing. [By analogy with righteous/righteousness]

**Right:** What made it even better was the **spontaneity** of the whole thing.

**Wrong:** I don't think he's incapable of doing it—he's just inwilling.

**Right:** I don't think he's incapable of doing it—he's just **unwilling**.

The second example above illustrates one of the most complicated prefixing rules in English: how to make an adjective negative. The following are all negative prefixes: ab-, il-, im-, in-, ir-, non, un-. The prefixes beginning with "i" vary depending on the way the adjective begins:

> in + capable = incapable
> in + prudent = imprudent
> in + regular = irregular
> in + legible = illegible

The un- prefix is invariable:

> un + professional = unprofessional
> un + manageable = unmanageable
> un + reliable = unreliable
> un + lawful = unlawful

While these rules are straightforward, the rules for whether to use un- or in- are more difficult; again, it is easier simply to learn the negative adjective form.

In addition, it is not safe to assume that the noun formed from the adjective will retain the same negative prefix.

| e.g. | just | unjust | injustice |
|------|------|--------|-----------|
|      | able | unable | inability |

**Wrong:** She is unable to accept responsibility: it is this unability that will limit her chances of promotion.

**Right:** She is **unable** to accept responsibility: it is this **inability** that will limit her chances of promotion.

Another potential problem with affixes is that some loss of vowels occurs when affixes are added in English.

**Wrong:** The links with the warring factions caused the company to disassociate itself from some lucrative deals.

**Right:** The links with the warring factions caused the company to **dissociate** itself from some lucrative deals.

**Wrong:** The patient complained to his psychiatrist about re-occurring nightmares.

**Right:** The patient complained to his psychiatrist about **recurring** nightmares.

Sometimes, however, both the form with the vowel and the form without exist, but with distinct meanings. For example, "disassemble" is the negative of "assemble"; the verb "dissemble," however, means to "disguise."

**Wrong:** Why are things always easier to dissemble than they are to assemble?

**Right:** Why are things always easier to **disassemble** than they are to assemble?

There are other words which appear to have a negative meaning, but do not:

**Wrong:** Why are you holding on to all that junk—it's invaluable.

**Right:** Why are you holding on to all that junk—it's **worthless**.

"Invaluable" is not the negative of "valuable"—in fact, it is a stronger form of "valuable," meaning "beyond value." "Priceless" poses similar problem: it might appear to have a negative meaning, but when something is priceless, it is so expensive that it is impossible to put a price on it.

Other adjectives have only a negative form: examples include "inert" and "inevitable." Other words should be used to express the meanings implied by the non-existent "ert" and "evitable."

**Wrong:** Death is inevitable, but I am sure everyone has thought at some point that they were immortal and that death was, in fact, evitable.

**Right:** Death is inevitable, but I am sure everyone has thought at some point that they were immortal and that death was, in fact, **avoidable**.

Another curious exception is the word "inflammable." It appears to be the negative form of "flammable," meaning "able to catch fire," while in fact the two words mean exactly the same. The negative form has to be "non-flammable."

Note that "non-flammable" is written with a hyphen. This raises the question of when a hyphen should be used with prefixes. Generally, a hyphen is not used unless the prefix is commonly accepted as a word by itself. Examples of this would be "self-awareness" and "well-known." However, hyphens are usually used on two occasions.

First, use a hyphen when the new word looks awkward because of clumsy spelling, e.g. "anti-institutional" or "pre-eminent." Other words containing a double vowel are often hyphenated, but this is often unnecessary.

**Poor:** The co-operation of all my co-workers has made the re-organization of the company much easier.

**Better:** The **cooperation** of all my co-workers has made the reorganization of the company much easier.

Second, a hyphen should be used when there is some ambiguity surrounding the newly formed words.

**Wrong:** I have to take my furniture to get it recovered.

**Right:** I have to take my furniture to get it **re-covered**.

**Wrong:** The cuts are so bad that the wounds will have to be redressed several times.

**Right:** The cuts are so bad that the wounds will have to be **re-dressed** several times.

Hyphens are used in adjectives when the adjective preceeds the noun (e.g. "the well-known film star"). However, when the adjective serves the role of predicate, a hyphen is not used (e.g. "the film star is well known").

# Two words or one?

A number of very commonly used English words have over many years become accepted as one word because they are combined so often. Other similar combinations, however, should still be written as two words. In a few cases one can see English usage changing on this point right now. A generation ago, for example, "alright" as one word could not have been found in any dictionary. Now a few authorities are beginning to regard "alright" as acceptable, and perhaps in another generation or two it will have completely replaced "all right." For the moment, though, it is best to stick with "all right" rather than the more colloquial "alright."

There are some pairs where the two-word and one-word forms have different meanings:

**all ready/already**: Use two words when using "all" with the adjective "ready." The adverb "already" has nothing to do with "ready."

> **Wrong:** Let's go to the dining room—dinner is already.
> **Right:** Let's go to the dining room—dinner is **all ready**.
> **But:** Dinner has **already** been served.

**all together/altogether**: Again, "altogether" is an adverb meaning "completely," while "all together" has an adjectival use.

> **Wrong:** He is not all together happy with the results.
> **Right:** He is not **altogether** happy with the results.
> **But:** They were **all together** when the results were announced.

**every day/everyday**: Two words are used when referring to time, while the adjective "everyday" must modify a noun.

> **Wrong:** To keep fit, I need to jog five miles everyday.
> **Right:** To keep fit, I need to jog five miles **every day.**
> **But:** For me, jogging is an **everyday** activity.

**every one/everyone**: "Everyone" is a noun form, while "every one" is typically followed by "of."

> **Wrong:** I can't decide which one to buy, so I think I'll take everyone of them.
> **Right:** I can't decide which one to buy, so I think I'll take **every one** of them.
> **But:** We don't know what to do—**everyone** is undecided.

**in to/into:** The latter is certainly used more often, but the former must be used when the meaning of in and to are not related. The same rule applies to "onto."

> **Wrong:** The police officer caught the thief trying to break in to the store.
> **Right:** The police officer caught the thief trying to break **into** the store.

**But:** The thief was trying to break **in to** steal all the stereos.

**may be/maybe:** "Maybe" means "perhaps," while "may be" is a verb form.

**Wrong:** He maybe here later tonight.
**Right:** He **may be** here later tonight.
**But:** **Maybe** he will be here later.

Other forms should only be written as two words:

| | | |
|---|---|---|
| a lot | every time | in fact |
| in order | in spite of | |
| in front | no one (or no-one) | |

**Wrong:** Everytime there is a full moon, people act strangely.
**Right:** **Every time** there is a full moon, people act strangely.

**Wrong:** I can't say it was my favourite play, but I liked it alot.
**Right:** I can't say it was my favourite play, but I liked it **a lot**.

Many more forms, however, should always be written as one word:

| | | |
|---|---|---|
| another | anybody | bathroom |
| bloodshed | businessman | cannot |
| anyone | bedroom | everybody |
| forever | furthermore | indeed |
| nearby | everything | ourselves |
| somebody | straightforward | wartime |
| whatever | myself | someone |
| whoever | yourself | nobody |
| however | | |

**Wrong:** Would you like an other drink?
**Right:** Would you like **another** drink?

**Wrong:** In a situation like this, one must brace one's self to face the worst.
**Right:** In a situation like this, one must brace **oneself** to face the worst.

The two-word choices above do not exist; in the sentences that follow, however, the two-word options have specific meanings.

**Wrong:** She is a great actor in deed.
**Right:** She is a great actor **indeed**.
**But:** She is a great hero, in thought and **in deed**.

> **Wrong:** Every body that was outside was sheltering from the rain.
> **Right:** **Everybody** that was outside was sheltering from the rain.
> **But:** **Every body** that was brought into the morgue was quite dead.

"Everybody" is synonymous with "everyone," while "every body" refers specifically to the noun "body" in its specific context.

# Infinitives, Gerunds, and Direct Objects

There are no rules in English to explain why some words must be followed by an infinitive ("to go," "to do," "to be," etc.), while others must be followed by a gerund ("of going," "in doing," etc.), and still others by a direct object. Here are some of the words with which difficulties of this sort most often arise.

**accept** something (*not* <u>accept to do something</u>)—needs a direct object

> **Wrong:** Michael Warren accepted to try to improve the quality of the postal service.
> **Right:** Michael Warren **accepted** the task of trying to improve the postal service.
> **Or:** Michael Warren agreed to try to improve the postal service.

**accuse** someone <u>of doing</u> something (*not* <u>to do</u>)

> **Wrong:** Klaus Barbie was accused to have killed thousands of innocent civilians in WW II.
> **Right:** Klaus Barbie was accused of having killed thousands of innocent civilians in WW II.

**appreciate** something: When used to mean "be grateful," this verb requires a direct object.

> **Wrong:** I would appreciate if you could respond quickly.
> **Right:** I would appreciate **it** if you could respond quickly.
> **Or:** I would appreciate a quick response.

(The verb "appreciate" without an object means "increase in value.")

**ask** someone to do something

> **Poor:** The official asked that we not smoke in the waiting room.
> **Better:** The official asked us not to smoke in the waiting room.

**assist** in doing something (*not* to do)

>Wrong: He assisted me to solve the problem.
>Right: He assisted me in solving the problem.
>Or: He helped me to solve the problem.

**capable** of doing something(*not* to do)

>Wrong: He is capable to run 1500 metres in under four minutes.
>Right: He is capable of running 1500 metres in under four minutes.
>Or: He is able to run 1500 metres in under four minutes.

**confident** of doing something

>Wrong: She is confident to be able to finish the job before dusk.
>Right: She is confident of being able to finish the job before dusk.
>Or: She is confident that she will finish the job before dusk.

**consider** something or someone to be something or consider them something (*not* as something)

>Wrong: According to a recent policy paper, the Party now considers a guaranteed annual income as a good idea.
>Right: According to a recent policy paper, the Party now considers a guaranteed annual income to be a good idea.
>Or: According to a recent policy paper, the Party now regards a guaranteed annual income as a good idea.

**discourage** someone from doing something (*not* to do)

>Wrong: The new Immigration Act is intended to discourage anyone who wants to come to Canada to enter the country illegally.
>Right: The new Immigration Act is intended to discourage anyone who wants to come to Canada from entering the country illegally.

**forbid** someone to do something (*not* from doing)

>Wrong: The witnesses were forbidden from leaving the scene of the crime until the police had completed their preliminary investigation.
>Right: The witnesses were forbidden to leave the scene of the crime until the police had completed their preliminary investigation.

**insist** on doing something *or* insist that something be done (but *not* insist to do)

> **Wrong:** The customer has insisted to wait in the front office until she receives a refund.
>
> **Right:** The customer has insisted on waiting in the front office until she receives a refund.

**intention**: Have an intention of doing something *but* someone's intention is/was to do something

> **Wrong:** Hitler had no intention to keep his word.
>
> **Right:** Hitler had no intention of keeping his word.
>
> **Or:** Hitler did not intend to keep his word.
>
> **Or:** Hitler's intention was to break the treaty.

**justified** in doing something (*not* to do something)

> **Wrong:** He is not justified to make these allegations.
>
> **Right:** He is not justified in making these allegations.

**look** forward to doing something (*not* to do something)

> **Wrong:** I am looking forward to receive your reply.
>
> **Right:** I am looking forward to receiving your reply.

**opposed** to doing something (*not* to do something)

> **Wrong:** He was opposed to set up a dictatorship.
>
> **Right:** He was opposed to setting up a dictatorship.
>
> **Or:** He was opposed to the idea of setting up a dictatorship.

**organize** something (*not* organize to do something)

> **Wrong:** We organized to meet at ten the next morning.
>
> **Right:** We organized a meeting for ten the next morning.
>
> **Or:** We arranged to meet at ten the next morning.

**persist** in doing something (*not* to do something)

> **Wrong:** Despite international disapproval and the will of Congress, the American administration persisted to help the contras in Nicaragua.
>
> **Right:** Despite international disapproval and the will of Congress, the American administration persisted in helping the contras in Nicaragua.

**plan** to do (*not* <u>on</u> doing)

> **Wrong:** They planned on closing the factory in Windsor.
> **Right:** They planned to close the factory in Windsor.

**prohibit** someone <u>from doing</u> something

> **Wrong:** Members of the public were prohibited to feed the animals.
> **Right:** Members of the public were prohibited from feeding the animals.

**regarded** <u>as</u> (*not* regarded <u>to be</u>)

> **Wrong:** He is commonly regarded to be one of Canada's best musicians.
> **Right:** He is commonly regarded as one of Canada's best musicians.

**responsible** <u>for doing</u> (*not* <u>to do</u>)

> **Wrong:** Mr Dumphy is responsible to market the full line of the company's pharmaceutical products.
> **Right:** Mr Dumphy is responsible for marketing the full line of the company's pharmaceutical products.

**sacrifice** <u>something</u>: The use of *sacrifice* without a direct object may have crept into the language through the use of the verb as a baseball term (e.g, "Olerud sacrificed in the ninth to bring home Alomar.").

> **Wrong:** He sacrificed to work in an isolated community with no electricity or running water.
> **Right:** He sacrificed himself to work in an isolated community with no electricity or running water.
> **Or:** He sacrificed a good deal; the isolated community he now works in has no electricity or running water.

**seem** <u>to be</u> (*not* <u>as if</u>)

> **Wrong:** The patient seemed as if he was in shock.
> **Right:** The patient seemed to be in shock.

*Exception*: When the subject is "it", "seem" can be followed by "as." (e.g., "It seemed as if he was sick, so we called the doctor.")

**suspect** someone <u>of doing</u> something (*not* <u>to do</u>)

**Wrong:** His wife suspected him to have committed adultery.
**Right:** His wife suspected him of committing adultery.
**Or:** His wife suspected that he had committed adultery.

**tell** someone to do something

**Wrong:** I told to the hyperactive student that he sit down and behave.
**Right:** I told the hyperactive student to sit down and behave.

**tendency** to do something (*not* of doing)

**Wrong:** Some Buick engines have a tendency of over-revving.
**Right:** Some Buick engines have a tendency to over-rev.
**Or** The engine has a habit of over-revving.

**want** someone to do something

**Wrong:** They want that we applaud after each group of names is called.
**Right:** They want us to applaud after each group of names is called.

**Wrong:** She wants that the boss step down so she can get her job.
**Right:** She wants the boss **to** step down so she can get her job.

# CAPITALIZATION

There are standard rules in English for what words should and should not be written with an initial capital letter. In general, English is quite strict about capitalization, especially where proper names, countries, and other "official" things are concerned.

The first word of every sentence always begins with a capital letter. This is an easy rule to remember; however, there are many other instances where a word is *always* capitalized. This category includes the following: countries, cities, and other geographical names; nationalities; names of people (and animals), both surnames and given names; days of the week and months of the year. The only personal pronoun to be capitalized is the first person singular pronoun "I." Note that the second person pronoun is never capitalized, even when used in a formal sense. The only exception to the rule is the third person singular "He" when referring to God.

**Wrong:** Dear Sir: I am writing to advise You that You have not paid Your bill, and that telephone service has been disconnected.

**Right:** Dear Sir: I am writing to advise **you** that **you** have not paid **your** bill, and that telephone service has been disconnected.

**Wrong:** Are you planning to call those young frenchmen you met last tuesday?

**Right:** Are you planning to call those young **Frenchmen** you met last **Tuesday?**

**Wrong:** All canadian people have a tendency to be depressed during the winter months, especially when suffering from the "february blues."

**Right:** All **Canadian** people have a tendency to be depressed during the winter months, especially when suffering from the "**February** blues."

In the second example above, the word "winter" is not capitalized. The seasons are typically not capitalized, although it is not unusual, especially in British English or in poetry, to see them capitalized.

Certain categories of words are capitalized in some cases, and not in others. The most obvious example of this is the category of people's titles. When a title—which refers to a person's occupation, rank, or position—is used with that person's name, it is usually capitalized because it becomes a part of the name. However, when used in a general sense, the word remains uncapitalized.

**Wrong:**    The last time I saw professor Rodriguez, she was at a party with sergeant Black and several military colonels.

**Right:**    The last time I saw **Professor** Rodriguez, she was at a party with **Sergeant** Black and several military colonels.

Note that the word "colonels" remains without capitalization because no name is mentioned. To remember this rule, try thinking of the titles like "Professor," "Doctor" and "Captain" as the same as more common personal titles like "Mister (Mr.)" and "Ms."

The general/specific distinction applies to other words too. Nouns which refer to geographical features like lakes and rivers, to buildings, institutions, etc., and to urban features like streets and crescents, are capitalized when used in a specific, particular sense. However, when they are used without a particular name, or when used generally, they remain uncapitalized.

**Wrong:**    The evidence shows that the pollution level of lake Ontario is much higher than that of other Lakes in the region.

**Right:**    The evidence shows that the pollution level of **Lake** Ontario is much higher than that of other lakes in the region.

**Wrong:**    I plan to attend a University in the United States—but it has to be close to Rivers and Mountains.

**Right:**    I plan to attend a university in the United States—but it has to be close to **rivers** and **mountains**.

**Wrong:**    The slightly crazy woman I saw on George street last week lives in one of the Avenues by the beach.

**Right:**    The slightly crazy woman I saw on George Street last week lives in one of the **avenues** by the beach.

As would be expected, when such words are used as adjectives, they lose their specificity and are not capitalized.

**Wrong:**    While serving as College Principal, she felt herself pulled in all directions by the demands of College business.

**Right:**    While serving as **college principal**, she felt herself pulled in all directions by the demands of **college** business.

**But:**    The **Principal** of the **College** came to all **college** functions.

**Wrong:**    It is clear that Lake levels close to these Mountain ranges have decreased significantly.

**Right:** It is clear that **lake** levels close to these **mountain** ranges have decreased significantly.

The main words of titles of books and other literary genres, as well as of films, television programs, and works of art and music, are capitalized. Within these titles, the articles, most prepositions, and other unimportant words are not capitalized.

**Wrong:** I intend to write a book review on Tolkien's *The Lord Of The Rings*.

**Right:** I intend to write a book review on Tolkien's *The Lord of the Rings*.

# SPELLING

The wittiest example of the illogicalities of English spelling remains Bernard Shaw's famous spelling of "fish" as "ghoti." The "gh" sounds like the "gh" in "enough;" the "o" sounds like the "o" in "women" (once spelled "wimmen," incidentally); and the "ti" sounds like the "ti" in "nation" or "station." Shaw passionately advocated a rationalization of English spelling; it still has not happened, and probably never will.

Perhaps the best way to learn correct spelling is to be tested by someone else, or to test yourself every week or so on a different group of words. For example, you might learn the words from the list below beginning with "a" and "b" one week, the words beginning with "c" and "d" the next week, and so on.

## Spelling and Sound

Many spelling mistakes result from similarities in the pronunciation of words with very different meanings. These are covered in the list below.

| | |
|---|---|
| absent (adjective) | absence (noun) |
| absorb | absorption |
| accept | except |
| access (entry) | excess (too much) |
| advice (noun) | advise (verb) |
| affect (to influence) | effect (result) |
| allowed (permitted) | aloud |
| alter (change) | altar (in a church) |
| appraise (value) | apprise (inform) |
| bitten | beaten |
| base (foundation) | bass (in music) |
| bath (noun) | bathe (verb) |
| believe (verb) | belief (noun) |
| berry (fruit) | bury (the dead) |
| beside (by the side of) | besides (as well as) |
| birth | berth (bed) |
| bizarre (strange) | bazaar (market) |
| bloc (political grouping) | block |
| breath (noun) | breathe (verb) |
| buoy (in the water) | boy |
| buy (purchase) | by |
| cash | cache (hiding place) |
| casual (informal) | causal (to do with causes) |

| | | |
|---|---|---|
| cause | case | |
| ceased (stopped) | seized (grabbed) | |
| ceiling (above you) | sealing | |
| chick | cheek | |
| chose (past tense) | choose (present tense) | |
| cite (make reference to) | sight | site |
| climatic | climactic | |
| cloths (fabrics) | clothes | |
| coma (unconscious) | comma (punctuation) | |
| compliment (praise) | complement (make complete) | |
| conscious (aware) | conscience (sense of right) | |
| contract | construct | |
| conventional (usual) | convectional | |
| conversation | conservation | concentration |
| cord (rope) | chord (music) | |
| convinced | convicted (of a crime) | |
| council (group) | counsel (advice) | |
| course | coarse (rough) | |
| credible (believable) | creditable (deserving credit) | |
| critic (one who criticises) | critique (piece of criticism) | |
| defer (show respect) | differ | |
| deference (respect) | difference | |
| deprecate (criticise) | depreciate (reduce in value) | |
| desert (dry place) | dessert (sweet) | |
| device (thing) | devise (to plan) | |
| died/had died | dead/was dead | |
| dissent (protest) | descent (downward motion) | |
| distant (adjective) | distance (noun) | |
| edition (of a book etc.) | addition (something added) | |
| emigrant | immigrant | |
| envelop (verb) | envelope (noun) | |
| except | expect | |
| fear | fair | fare (payment) |
| feeling | filling | |
| fell | feel | fill |
| flaunt (display) | flout | |
| formally | formerly (previously) | |
| forth (forward) | fourth (after third) | |
| forward | foreword (in a book) | |
| foul | fowl (birds) | |
| future | feature | |
| genus (biological type) | genius (creative intelligence) | |
| greet | great | grate (scrape) |
| guerillas | gorillas | |
| guided (led) | guarded (protected) | |

| | | |
|---|---|---|
| had | heard | head |
| heat | heart | hate |
| heir (inheritor) | air | |
| human | humane (kind) | |
| illicit (not permitted) | elicit (bring forth) | |
| illusion (unreal image) | allusion (reference) | |
| immigrate | emigrate | |
| independent (adjective) | independence (noun) | |
| inhabit (live in) | inhibit (retard) | |
| instance (occurrence) | instants (moments) | |
| intense (concentrating) | intents | |
| isle (island) | aisle (to walk in) | |
| know | no | now |
| kernel | colonel | |
| key | quay (wharf—pronounced key) | |
| lack | lake | |
| later | latter | letter |
| lath (piece of wood) | lathe (machine) | |
| lead | led | |
| leave | leaf | |
| leave | live | |
| leaving | living | |
| lessen (reduce) | lesson | |
| let | late | |
| liable (responsible) | libel (legal action) | |
| lightning (from clouds) | lightening (becoming lighter) | |
| lose (be unable to find) | loose (not tight) | |
| mad (insane) | made | maid (servant) |
| man | men | |
| marshal | martial (to do with fighting) | |
| mental | metal | |
| merry | marry | |
| met | meet | mate |
| minor (underage) | miner (underground) | |
| mist (light fog) | missed | |
| moral (ethical) | morale (spirit) | |
| mourning (after death) | morning | |
| new | knew | |
| of | off | |
| on | own | |
| ones | once | |
| pain | pane (of glass) | |
| patients (sick people) | patience (ability to wait) | |
| peer (look closely) | pier (wharf) | |
| perpetrate (be guilty of) | perpetuate (cause to continue) | |

| | | |
|---|---|---|
| perquisite (privilege) | prerequisite (requirement) | |
| personal (private) | personnel (employees) | |
| perspective (vision) | prospective (anticipated) | |
| poor | pour (liquid) | pore |
| precede (go before) | proceed (continue) | |
| precedent | president | |
| presents (gifts) | presence (being there) | |
| price (cost) | prize (reward) | |
| principle | principal (of a school) | |
| prostate | prostrate | |
| quite | quiet (not noisy) | |
| rein (to control animals) | rain | reign |
| release (let go) | realize (discover) | |
| relieve (verb) | relief (noun) | |
| response (noun) | responds (verb) | |
| rid | ride | |
| ridden | written | |
| rise | rice | |
| rite (ritual) | right | write |
| rod | rode | reared |
| rote (repetition) | wrote | |
| saved | served | |
| scene (location) | seen | |
| saw | so | sew |
| seam (in clothes etc.) | seem (appear) | |
| secret | sacred (holy) | |
| sell (verb) | sale (noun) | sail (boat) |
| senses | census (population count) | |
| shed | shade | |
| shone | shown | |
| shot | short | |
| sit | sat | set |
| smell | smile | |
| snake | snack (small meal) | |
| soar | sore (hurt) | |
| sole (single) | soul (spirit) | |
| sort (type or kind) | sought (looked for) | |
| stationery (paper) | stationary (not moving) | |
| steal (present tense) | stole (past tense) | |
| straight (not crooked) | strait (of water) | |
| striped (e.g., a zebra) | stripped (uncovered) | |
| suite (rooms or music) | suit | sweet |
| super | supper (meal) | |
| suppose | supposed to | |
| sympathies (noun) | sympathize (verb) | |

| | | |
|---|---|---|
| tale (story) | tail | |
| talk | took | |
| tap | tape | |
| than | then | |
| they | there | their |
| thing | think | |
| this | these | |
| throw | threw (past tense) | |
| through | thorough | |
| tied | tired | |
| urban (in cities) | urbane (sophisticated) | |
| vanish (disappear) | varnish | |
| vein (to carry blood) | vain | |
| vision (sight) | version | |
| waist (your middle) | waste | |
| wait | weight (heaviness) | |
| waive (give up) | wave | |
| wants | once | |
| weak (not strong) | week | |
| weather (sunny, wet, etc.) | whether (or not) | |
| wedding | weeding | |
| were | where | |
| wholly (completely) | holy (sacred) | holly |
| woman | women | |
| won | worn | |
| yoke (for animals) | yolk (of an egg) | |

# PUNCTUATION

This is a very brief guide to punctuation marks in English. Not designed to be a comprehensive survey of all uses of punctuation marks, it should provide some guidance as to the basic functions of punctuation, with special attention given to the apostrophe.

## The Period

The period (or full stop) marks the end of a complete sentence. A complete sentence expresses a complete thought: it should have at least a subject and a verb, and should not be a subordinate or relative clause without an accompanying main clause.

> **Wrong:** I never wear gloves in the winter. Which could be a reason for my poor health.
>
> **Right:** I never wear gloves in the winter, which could be a reason for my poor health.
>
> **Or:** I never wear gloves in the winter. This could be a reason for my poor health.

> **Wrong:** While Marina was walking to the sea and thinking of her father and the sound of a woodthrush.
>
> **Right:** While Marina was walking to the sea and thinking of her father and the sound of a woodthrush, she did not notice that she had lost her hat.

> **Wrong:** Unemployment is a serious problem in Canada. In fact, throughout the world.
>
> **Right:** Unemployment is a serious problem in Canada. In fact, it is a serious problem throughout the world.
>
> **Or:** Unemployment is a serious problem both in Canada and abroad.

The wrong sentences above are examples of sentence fragments or incomplete sentences, in which the period has been used where it does not belong.

## The Comma

Although the omission or wrong use of a comma sounds like a small mistake, it can be very important. The following group of words, for example, forms a sentence only if a comma is included.

**Wrong:** Because of the work that we had done before we were
ready to hand in the assignment.

**Right:** Because of the work that we had done before, we were
ready to hand in the assignment.

The omission or addition of a comma can also completely alter the meaning of a sentence—as it did in the Queen's University Alumni letter that spoke of the warm emotions still felt by alumni for "our friends, who are dead," (rather than "our friends who are dead"). The second would have been merely a polite remembrance of those Alumni who have died; the first suggests that *all* the friends of the reader are dead.

Commas very commonly come in pairs, and it is common as well to omit the second comma in a pair. Be particularly careful when putting commas around a name, or around an adjectival subordinate clause.

**Wrong:** My sister Caroline, has done very well this year in her
studies.

**Right:** My sister, Caroline, has done very well this year in her
studies.

**Wrong:** The snake which had been killed the day before, was
already half-eaten by ants.

**Right:** The snake, which had been killed the day before, was
already half-eaten by ants.

The corresponding error to the sentence fragment is the comma splice, where two main clauses are joined merely by a comma.

**Wrong:** I have found the materials I need in a small country shop,
but they are only open until 5:00, I am going there right
now.

**Right:** I have found the materials I need in a small country shop,
but they are only open until 5:00. I am going there right
now.

**Or:** I have found the materials I need in a small country shop,
but they are only open until 5:00, **so** I am going there
right now.

# The Question Mark

The question mark, naturally, follows a question, but only if that question is asked directly.

**Wrong:** The soldier asked what I was doing?

**Right:** The soldier asked what I was doing.
**Or:** The soldier asked "What are you doing?"

The wrong sentence would be right if the speaker were questioning whether or not "the soldier" asked a question about what the speaker was doing. This is not the same as a direct question being rephrased in indirect speech.

# The Exclamation Mark

This mark is used to give extremely strong emphasis to a statement. Most often used with the imperative mood ("Be gone!" "Sit!"), it should be used sparingly in other instances. It does not replace effective language if humour or satire is being sought; in fact, try to avoid using it unless absolutely necessary.

# The Semi-colon

The semi-colon is equivalent in usage to the period, but indicates a much closer relationship between what precedes the semi-colon and what follows it. Both sides of a semi-colon must be independent clauses, i.e. they must be able to stand alone. If the semi-colon cannot be replaced by a period, the semi-colon is incorrect.

**Wrong:** Much of Shakespeare's wit is lost on modern readers; because English has changed so much.
**Right:** Much of Shakespeare's wit is lost on modern readers, because English has changed so much.
**Or:** Much of Shakespeare's wit is lost on modern readers; English has changed so much, and many of his original meanings now appear to mean something much less humorous.

The semi-colon cannot be substituted for a colon.

**Wrong:** People are depressed these days for many reasons; the economy, the weather, and the fast pace of life.
**Right:** People are depressed these days for many reasons: the economy, the weather, and the fast pace of life.

The semi-colon can be used, however, after a colon to separate items in a list which have other punctuation.

**Poor:** I visited several places during the summer: Paris, Oslo, the capital of Norway, Venice, in Northern Italy, and New Delhi.

**Better:**   I visited several places during the summer: Paris; Oslo, the capital of Norway; Venice, in Northern Italy; and New Delhi.

# The Colon

The colon is used to introduce something that is either further information about what precedes the colon, a list pertaining to what precedes it, or an elaboration of a short title before the colon. It cannot be used interchangeably with a semi-colon, as described above, and it need not separate two independent clauses.

If introducing a list, be sure not to use a comma where a colon is required.

**Wrong:**   While shopping today, I bought four types of tropical fruit, papaya, guava, mango, and passion fruit.

**Right:**   While shopping today, I bought four types of tropical fruit: papaya, guava, mango, and passion fruit.

# The Dash

The dash (two hyphens typed together like this – –) can be used in two ways: first, in place of parentheses when the enclosed material is more important; and second, in place of a colon when a more emphatic introduction is needed.

**Right:**   I returned to Edinburgh (the city of my birth) to find it had changed a great deal.

**Better:**   I returned to Edinburgh—the city of my birth—to find it had changed a great deal.

**Right:**   He fainted when he heard how much he had won: one million dollars.

**Better:**   He fainted when he heard how much he had won—one million dollars.

# Parentheses

Parentheses are used to set off an interruption in the middle of a sentence, or to make a point which is not part of the main flow of the sentence. They are frequently used to give examples, or to express something in other words using the abbreviation "i.e." Example:

I found the poet's use of alliteration (i.e., the use of the same sound) very moving.

# The Apostrophe

The apostrophe is used in only two instances: possession and contraction.

## Possession

In English, possession can be indicated in one of three ways. First, a possessive pronoun like "my" can be used. Second, possession can be expressed using a prepositional phrase with "of." Third—and this is practically unique to English—possession can be indicated by an apostrophe.

An apostrophe is **never** used to indicate a plural.

Singular words form their possessive by adding the suffix -'s.

> **Wrong:** We have been asked to dinner by Harriets mother.
> **Right:** We have been asked to dinner by **Harriet's** mother.

Plurals have a few more options. When a plural ends in -s, the possessive is formed by adding an apostrophe only.

> **Wrong:** My two brother's wives are sisters, which is a strange coincidence.
> **Right:** My two **brothers'** wives are sisters, which is a strange coincidence.

However, plurals which end in a sound other than -s form their plural as if they were singular words.

> **Wrong:** When the ship went down, the womens' and childrens' lives were saved first.
> **Right:** When the ship went down, the **women's** and **children's** lives were saved first.

Singular nouns which end in -s can be problematic; this occurs especially with proper nouns indicating people's names. The truth is that either -'s or -' can be added, depending on preference. Consider how the word is actually pronounced.

> **Right:** President Stubbs's decision to accept another post came as a surprise to everyone.
> **Better:** President Stubbs' decision to accept another post came as a surprise to everyone.

> **Right:** Ray Charles' music has been very influential.

**Right:** Ray Charles's music has been very influential.

Noun phrases containing more than one word form their plural by adding the possessive marker to the last word in the phrase, and not necessarily to the noun which is the true possessor, as in "someone else's problem."

**Wrong:** The King's of England wife always becomes Queen, and the King's first son becomes the heir to the throne.

**Right:** The **King of England's** wife always becomes Queen, and the King's first son becomes the heir to the throne.

**Wrong:** Towards the end of the wedding reception, the master's of ceremonies voice was failing.

**Right:** Towards the end of the wedding reception, the master of **ceremonies'** voice was failing.

In the example above, the wrong response would sound like there were two masters of ceremonies; to avoid any ambiguity or confusion, the sentence could be rephrased as "... the M.C.'s voice was failing" (using an abbreviation) or "... the master of ceremonies was losing his voice."

When two or more people are possessors, a distinction must be made between joint and separate possession: if the thing possessed belongs to both at once, the possessive marker is added to the end of the phrase; if, however, separate ownership (perhaps of two distinct things or things in different historical periods) is suggested, possession markers are needed after each possessor.

**Wrong:** Our daughter attends ballet classes with Andrew's and Sarah's elder daughter.

**Right:** Our daughter attends ballet classes with Andrew and **Sarah's** elder daughter.

**Wrong:** There are major differences between Mozart and Tchaikovsky's symphonies.

**Right:** There are major differences between **Mozart's** and **Tchaikovsky's** symphonies.

Because the "of" form of possession is used more with inanimate objects than with people, there are cases where both "of" and -'s are used to mark the possession of something by a person.

**Poor:** Remember that bike of Jeff that I was riding last week? Well I want one.

**Better:** Remember that bike of **Jeff's** that I was riding last week? Well I want one.

With personal pronouns, a similar thing happens; in such cases, of course, the possessive pronoun is used instead of the possessive adjective.

> **Wrong:** Look at the dog-eared corners! This is no book of my.
> **Right:** Look at the dog-eared corners! This is no book of **mine**.

## Contraction

Contraction is very common in informal English. However, it is practically avoided in formal, written English, although its clever incorporation in a formal piece can add some much-needed levity. The apostrophe is used to show the absence of a vowel from words like "not," "have," and "will" when combined with another word, often an auxiliary verb or personal pronoun. Some examples follow:

| Original word | Contraction | Complete form |
|---|---|---|
| not | can't | cannot |
| | don't | do not |
| | isn't | is not |
| is/has | it's | it is/has |
| | that's | that is/has |
| would/had | I'd | I would/had |
| | we'd | we would/had |
| | you'd | you would/had |
| am | I'm | I am |
| are | you're | you are |
| | we're | we are |
| have | I've | I have |
| | they've | they have |
| will/shall | I'll | I will/shall |
| | we'll | we will/shall |
| | she'll | she will/shall |

Certain contractions should be avoided since they sound clumsy; they also defeat the purpose of contraction by not making the phrase any easier to say.

> **Wrong:** Your boyfriend may stay the night, but he mayn't sleep in the same room!
> **Right:** Your boyfriend may stay the night, but he **may not** sleep in the same room!

> **Wrong:** There're many long nights to go before spring.
> **Right:** **There are** many long nights to go before spring.

> **Wrong:** I'm in trouble this time, amn't I?
> **Right:** I'm in trouble this time, **aren't** I?

The tag question above is an example of very colloquial language. Because of its nature it would rarely appear in written form; "aren't" has come to replace "amn't" because it is easier to say, in the same way as the equally colloquial "ain't" often replaces "isn't."

# SPECIFIC LANGUAGE DIFFICULTIES

The exercises which follow this chapter make some specific references to certain problem areas in various languages and language groups. While some of the exercises have instructions which appear to limit their applicability, **all** exercises can be attempted by **all** readers. This section deals in summary form with some of the particular problem areas of English, and then goes on to detail some of the problems that specific languages and language groups will encounter.

## The Problems of English

There are several problem areas in which second language learners will encounter difficulties. The major ones are listed here:

- A complicated system of tenses with forms like "I would like to have been able to be doing" and very specific meanings for each tense

- Numerous auxiliaries to express negation, interrogation, and to emphasize declarative sentences: "I do not like"; "Do you like?"; "I do like"

- Progressive tenses which can often not be used interchangeably with their simple equivalents: "She plays the harpsichord" vs. "She is playing the harpsichord"

- Definite and indefinite articles are used considerably less frequently than in most languages, and they are even more problematic for speakers of languages that have no articles

- English has no grammatical gender, but it does have a neuter personal pronoun, "it"

- Adjectives do not agree with the nouns they qualify, but occupy a certain position within the sentence; adverbs also belong in a particular position

- The language has a particularly confusing and illogical system of prepositions which more than compensates for its lack of ostensible grammatical case declension

- Prepositions combine with verbs to produce a unique breed of linguistic problem called the "phrasal verb"

- English combines two techniques for creating comparatives and superlatives:

sometimes both can be used, sometimes only one or the other

Direct object pronouns follow the usual English word order, but can occasionally move: "I gave the suitcase to him"; "I gave him the suitcase"

- Word order itself is quite strictly subject-verb-object, with a few exceptions

- Double and triple negatives, familiar and permissible in other languages, are not accommodated in English

- Certain words must be followed by an infinitive, others by a gerund, and others by a direct object: there appear to be no rules to govern the choice

# Problems of specific languages and language groups

It is always difficult (and dangerous) to classify languages, since the very act if classification begins to destroy the uniqueness that makes languages exist as independent languages. However, languages are indeed classified in order to identify the common links between related languages. Linguists use this information to trace etymologies, and to reconstruct dead languages and ancient cultures. For the purposes of this book, it is useful to look at how certain languages share common aspects which lead to common problems and, ultimately, to common errors in the use of English.

The general exercises at the end of the book create three divisions: Oriental, including Cantonese, Japanese, and Vietnamese; Slavic, which covers Russian, Polish, Serbo-Croat, Bulgarian, etc.; and Romance, which includes French, Spanish, Italian, Romanian, and Portuguese. While these groupings are not exclusive and could be criticized for over-simplifying linguistic diversity, there are sufficient common elements to make some generalizations which are useful at this stage. Taking its lead from the previous section, this short section will detail some of the major problem areas each of these three groups will face. The exercises at the end complement these explanations.

## Oriental and Far Eastern Languages

- Most languages in this group do not have definite or indefinite articles. This leads to a tendency to omit them or, as a result of over-compensation, to add too many.

- Verbs tend not to be conjugated for one or more of the following: person, number, tense. Because of this, speakers of such languages are likely to construct English sentences without -s on third person singular forms, without past tense markers, and so forth. Again, there is a risk of hypercorrection.

- Word order is extremely important because of the lack of verb conjugation and noun declension. This leads to a rather rigid approach to the placement of various parts of speech. Errors occur frequently in the positioning of adverbs, verbs, and adjectives.

- The concept of the infinitive form is difficult to grasp; some speakers will add tense or person markers to the infinitive, e.g. "It was difficult to felt ...."

- Personal pronouns are either highly complicated or not important in these languages. Both extremes lead to usage problems, especially with "he," "she," and "you."

- The plural form of nouns is rarely expressed.

- A complex system of particles leads to confusion in such areas as prepositions, negation, interrogation, and possession.

## Slavic Languages

- Slavic languages have complex systems of noun declension which permit a rather loose word order. This leads to the most common problem these speakers face, i.e., not following the rules of English word order. As in Oriental languages, this affects adverbs, verbs, and adjectives, as well as the position of direct and indirect objects.

- The number of verb tenses tends to be quite limited, resulting in a poor understanding of the complexity of verb tense distinctions in English. The present perfect tense is particularly troubling, but the verb systems usually do distinguish between perfective and imperfective aspects.

- Definite and indefinite articles are rarely expressed in these languages.

- The copulative verb "be" either does not exist or is not used to the same extent as in English. A common error is the simple subject-predicate construction like "He teacher, she engineer."

- Double negatives are permissible; simple negative particles are used to form the negative.

- Possessive pronouns and possessive adjectives, distinguished in English, tend to be identical in Slavic languages.

- As in many other languages, the relative pronouns "who" and "which" are not distinguished in Slavic languages.

- There is a common technique of infixing employed to form the comparative and superlative forms of the adjective.

- The distinctions between "much" and "many," and "few" and "little" are not clear to Slavic speakers. This presents problems with countable and uncountable nouns.

## Romance Languages

- Adjectives can often be placed after the nouns they qualify, something which is rare in English.

- Romance languages have only one method of forming comparatives and superlatives: "more big" is the typical model, with forms like "bigger" being unfamiliar.

- There is confusion between animate and inanimate forms of the relative pronoun, i.e., "who" and "which." In addition, the words for "that" and "what" are often not distinguished.

- There are strict rules for the position and order of object pronouns in sentences. While the strictness itself is not problematic, the rules are not followed in English. In most Romance languages, object pronouns precede the verb.

- Reflexive verbs are more common, often expressing concepts for which English does not require a reflexive.

- Particles, not auxiliaries, are used to form negatives and interrogatives.

- Double negatives are permissible.

- While word order is often parallel, the position of adverbs can fluctuate greatly.

- The present tense is often used for the future in constructions like "Tomorrow I come to see you."

- Articles tend to be over-used in English translations of Romance sentences. There is particular overuse of the definite article.

- With the exception of Spanish, progressive tenses do not exist. This leads to problems in constructing sentences which require a distinction between simple and progressive tenses.

- Although grammatical gender does not pose too many problems in itself, it affects possession. Possessive adjectives agree with what is possessed, and not with who is possessing. A distinction like that between "her dog" and "his dog" would not exist.

For some of the material in this chapter, we would like to acknowledge the authors of "Thirteen Language Profiles: Practical Application of Contrastive Analysis for Teachers of English as a Second Language" (Vancouver Community College, 1983).

# LANGUAGE AND GENDER

**Sexist language.** The healthy revolution in attitudes towards gender roles in the last generation has created some awkwardness in English usage — though not nearly so much as some have claimed. "Chairperson," or even simply "chair" is an unobjectionable non-sexist replacement for "chairman," as is "business people" for" businessmen," and "humanity" may serve for "mankind." Nor is one forced into "garbageperson" or "policeperson"; "police officer" and "garbage collector" are entirely unobjectionable even to the linguistic purist. "Fisher" is a quite delightful replacement for "fisherman"; here again, there is no need for a "-person" suffix. The use of "mankind" to mean "humanity," and of "man" to mean "human being" have for some years been rightly frowned upon. (Ironically enough, "man" originally had "human being" as its <u>only</u> meaning; in Old English a "werman" was a male adult human being, a "wifman" a female.)

The nouns are gradually sorting themselves out; the pronouns are more difficult. Clearly the consistent use of "he" to represent both sexes is unacceptable. Yet "he/she," "s/he," or "he or she" are undeniably awkward. "S/he" is quite functional on the printed page, but defies translation into oral English. Another solution is to avoid the singular pronoun as much as possible either by repeating nouns ("An architect should be aware of the architect's clients' budgets as well as the architect's grand schemes") or by switching to the plural ("Architects should be aware of their clients' budgets as well as of their own grand schemes"). Of these two the second is obviously preferable. In longer works some prefer a third strategy that eliminates awkwardness entirely: to alternate between the masculine pronoun "he" and the feminine pronoun "she" when referring to a single, generic member of a group. Using "she" to refer to, say, an architect, or a professor, or a sports star, or a prime minister can have the salutary effect of reminding readers or listeners that there is nothing inherently male in these occupations. In a short piece of writing, however, it can be distracting to the reader if there are several bounces back and forth between female and male in the same paragraph. And a cautionary note should accompany this strategy even when it may conveniently be employed; be *very* careful not to assign "he" to all the professors, executives, or doctors; and "she" to all the students, secretaries, or nurses.

Undoubtedly the most troublesome questions for those who are concerned both about gender equality and about good English arise over situations involving singular pronouns such as "everyone," "anyone," "anybody," "somebody, someone, no one," "each," "either," "neither." It can be difficult enough to re-cast sentences involving such words so that everything agrees even before the issue of gender enters the picture.

Everybody felt that the film was better than any other

they had seen that year.

According to the grammatical rules most of us have been taught, that sentence is wrong; "everybody" is singular, and "they" must therefore be changed:

> Everybody felt that the film was better than any other she had seen that year.

> Everybody felt that the film was better than any other he had seen that year.

> Everybody felt that the film was better than any other she or he had seen that year.

But, as Robertson Cochrane has pointed out ("Sex and the Single Pronoun," *The Globe and Mail*, May 1992), the insistence on the singularity of such pronouns is a relatively recent phenomenon, dating from the codification of English grammar that took root in the eighteenth century. Before that time Chaucer, Shakespeare, Swift, and the rest had no qualms about using "they" or "their" to refer to "anyone" and "everyone." Cochrane persuasively argues that returning to the ways of Chaucer and Shakespeare in this respect is better than constantly trying "to write around the pronoun problem, and [it is] certainly less offensive than arrogantly and 'properly' applying masculine labels to all of humankind."

**inappropriate:**

> Mankind cannot bear too much reality.

**gender neutral:**

> Human kind cannot bear too much reality.

**inappropriate (though 'correct'):**

> Everyone will have a chance to express his views before the meeting is over.

**gender neutral (though 'incorrect'):**

> Everyone will have a chance to express their views before the meeting is over.

# EXERCISES

# PART I: Exercises on specific grammatical points

### Exercise I: Simple present tense/plural markers

The suffix -s can mark both the third person singular form and regular plurals. This can be problematic for speakers of languages which do not have separate verb forms, like **Cantonese** and **Japanese**, and in languages like **Vietnamese** which do not indicate plurality.

Add an *s* where necessary to plural nouns, third person singular verbs, etc.

1.  Train in Burma usually run on time, although it sometime take many hours to get from one place to another. The trip from Belowa to Rangoon, for example, last about eleven hour. The Railway Corporation use several different type of locomotive- steam, electric, and diesel. The newest are the electric locomotive that travel between Rangoon and Mutisa.

2.  Most of the electricity that the State need come from the dam. When the water flow over the large turbine, it turn them and this produce large amount of electricity.

3.  When a debate start, the Chairman alway introduce the topic and then three speaker from each team argue for or against the resolution. Each speaker talk for several minute. At the end of the debate the Chairman give anyone in the crowd who wish to speak a chance to do so.

4.  In politic as in everyday life the variation that interest us occur in two dimension. Sometime political scientist are curious about variation over time. For instance, they may ask why the number of vote received by the various parties fluctuate so much from one election to the next. At other time political scientist concentrate their attention on variation over space. They may be interested, for example, in why one nation government seem to enjoy more success than it neighbour in combatting inflation, or protecting human right.

### Exercise 2: Simple present tense and subject pronouns

Many languages express the personal pronoun subject within the verb form itself, unlike English where the subject must be expressed. While this exercise is useful for all speakers, it will be especially appropriate for speakers of **Spanish**, **Italian**, **Portuguese**, and **Serbo-Croatian**, among others.

Insert the appropriate personal pronoun subject and the appropriate form of the verb in the following sentences:

1. _____ soccer for the local team every Saturday. [my brother and I, play]

2. _____ long hours every spring doing our taxes. [my husband and his accountant, spend]

3. While _____ dinner every night, _____ the paper. [my cousin, cook; his wife, read]

4. _____ to every word _____ during the lecture. [the students, listen; the professor, say]

## Exercise 3: Subject-verb agreement

Correct the subject-verb agreement error in each of the following:

1. Fowler (1962) pointed out that concern about the dangers of premature cognitive training and an overemphasis on personality development had delayed inordinately the recognition that the ability to talk, read and compute increase the child's self-respect and independent functioning.

2. Canada's chances of making it to the televised finals, where the big payoff to sponsors come, are not great. (*Financial Post*, Nov. 23, 1987)

3. To make matters worse, none of the three in the Leafs' training camp have much playoff experience. (*Toronto Star*, Sept. 20, 1991)

4. The technical aspect of the newspaper has also been re-evaluated. Typos, or mistakes in spelling and grammar, which makes comprehension difficult, has been made almost a thing of the past. (Editorial in *The Statesman*, student newspaper of the State University of New York at Stony Brook, as quoted in *The New Yorker*, Jan. 12, 1992.)

## Exercise 4: Simple present tense revisited

Fill in the correct form of the simple present tense in the following passages, and notice how the present progressive cannot be used.

EXERCISES

1. Every day the sun _____[to rise] in the east and
_____[to set] in the west. Because of this, some people
_____[to think] that the sun _____[to revolve]
around the earth. In fact, the opposite _____[to be] true; the
earth _____[to circle] the sun once every day. While the sun
_____[to shine] on one side of the earth, it _____[to be]
night on the other side.

2. This year she _____[to follow] the same pattern of teaching
in many lessons. As soon as she _____[to come] into the class
she _____[to ask] several questions on the previous day's
work. Then she usually _____[to introduce] a new topic,
and _____[to talk] to us about it for several minutes. More
often than not she then _____[to assign] a written exercise
to do in class. If the students _____[to finish] the exercise
before the end of the class, she _____*[to correct]* it on the
board. Sometimes if there _____[to be] a few minutes remain-
ing she _____[to tell] a story or asks a student to tell a story.

3. Shylock _____[to be] the most important character in Shakespeare's *The Merchant of Venice*. We _____[to sympathize]
with him despite his streak of cruelty, because we_____[to
be made] to understand his resentment against the Christians. When
Shylock _____[to accuse] Antonio in Act One of having
sworn at him and spat on him merely because of his religion, Antonio—far from denying the charges—_____[to say] that he would
do the same again. Moreover, Antonio's prejudice against Jews
_____[to seem] to be shared by all the Christian characters
in the play.

## Exercise 5: "To be"

Fill in the correct form of the verb "to be" in the simple present tense in the
following sentences.

1. We _____ happy that you could make it.

2. _____ the people you met as enthusiastic about this as you
_____?

3. My sister and I _____ probably friendlier now than we ever
were.

4. A puppy _____ one of the best companions a human can have.

5. Neither of my aunts _____ able to attend my wedding.

6. _____ this an indication of the way things _____ in this country all the time?

## Exercise 6: Simple present vs. present progressive

English is one of the few languages in the world to have progressive tenses. **Spanish** has an equivalent, but it is not used to the extent that the progressive is used in English. Fill in the correct simple present or present progressive form of the verb in the following passages.

1. Many soldiers _____ [fight] in Somalia right now. It _____ [appear] to some people that the war that _____ [go on] there _____ [interfere] with the attempts to get food to the starving.

2. When the phone _____ [ring], I _____ [answer] it most of the time, unless I _____ [feel] tired, in which case I _____ [put] the answering machine on. Tonight I _____ [not answer] it, so please don't call.

3. In Euripides' play, Herakles _____ [return] home to find that his wife and children _____ [hide] from the evil tyrant who _____ [want] to kill them. Herakles _____ [kill] the tyrant, but later, in a fit of madness, _____ [kill] his family himself.

4. I _____ [look for] a way to write this essay in an interesting way. I _____ [hate] writing essays but my professor _____ [expect] me to improve upon my last effort. He _____ [try] to make good writers out of us.

5. Look! The plane _____ [take off]. Planes _____ [take off] and _____ [land] here every day. Hundreds of people _____ [be] in the air right now, and I _____ [bet] even more _____ [arrive] and _____ [depart] this very minute. I _____ [like] flying, and I _____ [look forward] to my next trip.

## Exercise 7: Simple present vs. present perfect (simple and progressive)

Many languages—**French** and **Russian** among them—use the simple present tense in expressions of time involving "since" and "for." English, of course, uses the present perfect. Use the correct tense of the verb in the sentences below.

1. Since 1986, I _____ [work] for the local firefighters on a volun-

teer basis.

2.   The boys _____ [be] unhappy ever since their father left home.

3.   For many years now, medical researchers _____ [look for] clues to find cures for the common cold.

4.   The teacher _____ [not teach] since her operation last year.

5.   I _____ [not talk] about the accident with anyone since we discussed it last week.

6.   My sister _____ [play] the guitar since she was four.

7.   For years now I _____ [try] to discover the secrets that he _____ [hide] from me.

8.   For how many years you _____ [follow] the author across the world?

## Exercise 8: Simple past vs. present perfect (simple and progressive)

Distinguishing between the uses of the simple past tense and the present perfect tense can often be difficult. Fill in the correct past form of the verb in the sentences below.

1.   I _____ [write] a tragedy for my drama class this week, modelled on the great plays of Sophocles, who _____ [write] many tragedies in ancient Greece.

2.   I am climbing the tree because my cat _____ [disappear].

3.   Last week, I _____ [exercise] every day; this week, because of my cold, I _____ [not exercise] at all.

4.   When my brother was a young boy, he _____ [get] into trouble a lot; he is relieved that, so far, his son Matt _____ [not get] into any trouble—yet.

5.   The office assistant _____ [copy] the documents you _____ [give] him. Can he go home now since he _____ [come] in early this morning?

6.   I _____ [not be able] to hear properly since I _____ [fall] from my horse last Saturday.

### Exercise 9: Simple past vs. past perfect

Choose the correct past tense form of the verb in the following sentences.

1.  The doctor _____ [come] just after you _____ [leave].

2.  When he _____ [ask], I told him what you _____ [say].

3.  After the journalist _____ [arrive] in Buenos Aires, she _____ [find out] what _____ [happen].

4.  Before the boys _____ [arrive] in Canada, they _____ [never see] snow.

5.  I _____ [not read] the discussion paper when I _____ [go] to the meeting.

6.  When I _____ [marry] Joan, she _____ [know] that I _____ [have] three wives before.

7.  John _____ [eat] his dinner before the police _____ [come] to take him away.

8.  The scientists _____ [try] numerous methods when they suddenly _____ [hit] upon the solution.

### Exercise 10: Future tense

In the following complex sentences (i.e. with a main clause and a subordinate clause), use a future tense in the appropriate clause and choose the correct tense for the other clause.

1.  I _____ [paint] the entire house by the time you _____ [return].

2.  When you _____ [be] 16, you _____ [be able] to start driving lessons.

3.  The early morning radio announcer _____ [do] a full day's work before you _____ [get up].

4.  When we _____ [win] the lottery, we _____ [quit] our jobs and _____ [travel] the world.

5.  I _____ [stop] screaming as soon as you _____ [stop] frightening me.

6.   We _____ [celebrate] with champagne and caviar when we finally _____ [finish] the renovations.

## Exercise 11: The Conditional

Fill in either the conditional tense or the simple future tense in the main clause.

Example

I [to help] him if I could.

I would help him if I could. (conditional)

1.   If I found someone's wallet lying on the ground, I [to return] it.

2.   If I find the wallet that you have lost, I [to return] it.

3.   You [to find] the weather extremely cold if you lived at the North Pole.

4.   You [to find] the weather extremely cold when you come to Canada this coming January.

5.   If he gets here before three o'clock, I [to take] him to see the museum.

6.   If you were the Prime Minister, what _____you_____ [to do] about the situation?

7.   I [to be] very happy if the company hires me as an apprentice.

8.   If I were very rich, I [to buy] a house in West Vancouver.

Fill in either the simple past or the simple present tense in the subordinate clause:

9.   I will ask him about it if I _____ [to see] him again later today.

10.   If I _____ [to win] the lottery I will buy my parents a new car.

11.   If I _____ [to win] the lottery I would buy my parents a new car.

12.   He would do better if he _____ [to work] harder.

13.   He will do better if he _____ [to work] harder next term.

14. If a burglar _____ [to come] into your room at night, what would you do?

15. I will lend you my typewriter if you _____ [to promise] to take good care of it.

16. She would look quite pretty if she _____ [to arrange] her hair differently.

17. There can no longer be any doubt that people _____ [to live] longer if they [to smoke] less.

## Exercise 12: Conditional sentences

Fill in the missing verbs.

1. He _____[to supply] our company with what we need if we _____[to pay] him $50,000. However, we only _____[to have] $30,000 in liquid assets.

2. If he _____[to reply] to me quickly, as I think he will, I _____[to be able] to make reservations for our holiday.

3. If she _____[to believe] in God she _____[to go] to church. However, she _____[to be] an atheist.

4. My friend and I are thinking of going to the game this afternoon. If we _____[to go] we probably _____[to take] our wives with us.

5. If we _____[to arrive] sooner, we would have been able to help him.

6. If Montcalm's most important officer _____not_____[to be hiding] away with his mistress, the French troops _____[to be assembled] earlier and the British _____[to lose] the battle on the Plains of Abraham.

7. We would have been better off if we _____[to plant] wheat instead of cotton.

8. If you had spoken to me about it, I _____[to do] something sooner.

9. I would have told them the truth if they _____[to ask] me.

10. The Titanic _____probably not _____[to sink] if it had struck the iceberg head on.

## Exercise 13: Conditional sentences

Complete the following sentences in any appropriate way.

1. If I wore no clothes at all...

2. If South Africa eliminates apartheid...

3. He would buy a truck if...

4. He will buy a truck if...

5. If an election is held next month...

6. She will win if...

7. She would win if...

8. If money were abolished...

9. Local farms would be more productive if...

10. If he sends me the money in time...

## Exercise 14: The Subjunctive

Although the subjunctive is not used much in English, it has several important applications. Use the subjunctive or the indicative, as appropriate, in the sentences below.

1. If I _____ [be] older, I would be able to do all sorts of things, like drink, get married, ... and pay bills.

2. If I _____ [be] bored in a big city, I would head for the nearest bookstore.

3. The travel agent recommended that she _____ [leave] for the airport at least three hours before the flight.

4. He understands that we _____ [be] unable to attend because of a prior engagement.

5. I suggest that you _____ [be] on your best behaviour tonight if

you want to impress the director of that new film.

## Exercise 15: Forming negative statements

English has a peculiar way of forming negatives. Speakers of **all** languages should try the following exercise and become more familiar with the use of the auxiliary "do" when making a sentence negative; this is very different from the negative particles that most other languages have.

Make the following sentences negative.

1. I believe in allowing children to decide what they should do in the classroom because it lets them become more independent.

2. Caffeine in coffee is more powerful than caffeine found in tea; if given the choice, I would drink coffee.

3. If I were able to see without my glasses, I could wear regular sunglasses when I am driving.

4. Ted played rugby when he was young because he thought it would make him fit and strong.

5. If the orchestra played quietly, the opera singers would be able to be heard clearly.

## Exercise 16: Double negatives

Languages like **Russian** and **Polish**, and **Spanish** and **Italian** allow a number of negatives together within sentences. Speakers of these languages—and others—should try to avoid double and triple negatives in English.

Correct the following multiple negatives.

1. We don't know of no way we can get around the problem.

2. I cannot never get to know her because she never says nothing to nobody in class.

3. No library services are not available today because of the holiday.

4. Don't repeat a word of this to nobody!

5. She hardly does nothing when she is not constantly supervised.

6. Neither of her sons could not read or write nothing.

## Exercise 17: Questions

English has some very particular ways of forming interrogative statements; this exercise is valuable for speakers of **all** languages. Make the following declarative sentences into questions that would require a yes/no response. (Remember to change pronouns where necessary.)

1. The lava is flowing very quickly down the side of the volcano.

2. The people in the villages were afraid that a major eruption would happen soon.

3. We expect the year ahead to be more prosperous.

4. The weight of the dictionaries caused the shelf to break.

5. I eat clams and squid at least three times a week.

6. You look like my brother.

## Exercise 18: Interrogative and Imperative Statements

Wh- words are the common question words in English: what, who, which, where, when, why, and how. In response to the following statements, ask a wh- question, then rephrase the question beginning with the command "Tell me..." For example:
Statement:The helicopter tour is leaving at 5:00.

Question:**When is** the helicopter tour leaving?

Command:Tell me **when** the helicopter tour **is** leaving.

Another question is possible:

Question:**What** is leaving at 5:00?

Command:Tell me **what** is leaving at 5:00.

1. My car is serviced every three months, without fail.

2. The best way to get rid of mice is to buy a cat.

3. In mid-June, the sun appears to rise very close to the north.

4. I prefer the blue shirt with the button-down collar.

5.   People like to ski because of the exhilarating sensation of gliding down the slopes.

6.   Margaret Thatcher was Britain's first female Prime Minister.

## Exercise 19: Tag questions

Most languages have a single word or expression which can be added to a declarative statement to make it into a type of question. In **French**, "n'est-ce pas?" is used, in **Japanese** "ka?" is added to the end of the sentence, and in **Russian** "da?" or "nye pravda li?" is the tag question marker. They are invariable, which makes them easy to use. English has variable tag question phrases. Add a tag question to the following statements.

1.   The workers are repairing the potholes on Water Street.

2.   He is not going to cooperate with us.

3.   I won't be fired for this.

4.   You're not actually suggesting that I eat this.

5.   If today is the winter solstice, that means the days start getting longer.

6.   People used to lead much less stressful lives.

## Exercise 20: Dangling constructions

Correct the following sentences:

1.   Riding the bus to work, his wife waved at him from the sidewalk.

2.   When covered with aluminum siding, we will have a much more salable house.

3.   Regarding the fiscal requirements of the government, an increase in taxes will be required if the deficit is to be reduced.

4.   Looking for a moment at the implications of Smith's argument, he allows us to justify our selfish behavior.

5.   Having covered the issue of stratification, the means of redistributing income will be dealt with next.

6.   To obtain a sense of the density of structuralist prose, a few exam-

ples should suffice.

7. We have asked for a survey of the attitudes of consumers carried out randomly.

8. Considering all of this evidence, there is no doubt that an increased awareness of the usefulness of uniform and objectively-defined time led to the spread of clocks, and not the other way round.

9. Widely regarded as a failure by observers at the time, we can now see that Truman was a remarkably successful president.

10. To begin this essay, Faulkner's novel is written from several points of view.

## Exercise 21: Irregular verbs

Correct whichever of the following are incorrect:

1. She can do whatever she choses.

2. The book is well-written and beautifully layed out.

3. He says that he rung me over the phone.

4. They have stole everything I own.

5. This blouse shrunk when I washed it in hot water.

6. The ship sunk in a hundred metres of water.

Fill in the simple past tense of the verbs indicated:

1. She _____ (to choose) the material that _____ (to be) least expensive.

2. Samuel _____ (to drink) too much beer last night.

3. All the pipes _____ (to burst) and water covered the floor.

4. The little baby _____ (to fall) asleep as soon as he _____ (to lie) down.

5. The soldiers _____ (to flee) as soon as they _____ (to see) the size of the opposing force.

6.   As soon as I apologised, my parents _____ (to forgive) me.

7.   We _____ (to grind) the seeds into a fine powder.

8.   He _____ (to lay) his book down for a moment, and then he _____ (to forget) where he had put it.

9.   I _____ (to lend) him five dollars yesterday.

10.  The letter carrier _____ (to ring) the bell four times.

11.  His whole family _____ (to seek) refuge here after leaving El Salvador.

12.  The moon _____ (to shine) very brightly last night.

13.  The bandits _____(to shoot) the policeman in the back.

14.  This sweater _____ (to shrink) when I washed it in hot water.

15.  He _____ (to sing) at the top of his voice all afternoon.

16.  When the *Titanic* _____ (to sink), over 1,500 lives _____ (to be) lost.

17.  All my food _____ (to slide) off my plate onto the floor.

18.  He _____ (to spend) his entire wages on beer and cigarettes.

19.  The car _____ (to spin) out of control as it _____ (to go) around the corner.

20.  He _____ (to spit) in disgust on the pavement.

21.  She _____ (to split) the log into two easily.

22.  The cougar _____ (to spring) out of the undergrowth at the deer.

23.  We _____ (to swim) in the pool below the falls.

24.  She _____ (to weep) for hours when she _____ (to hear) the sad news.

25.  The python _____ (to wind) itself around his neck.

26. He _____ (to wring) out the wet clothing, and put it on the line.

## Exercise 22: Direct/Indirect Speech

Correct the errors in the indirect (reported) speech that stems from the conversation below.

"You can come with me to the game tomorrow," the man said to is son, "as long as you clean the car first."

The boy replied, "Great. When I'm older, I'll be cleaning the car and driving it, and then I might let you come to the game with me."

"I'll be too old and embarrassing for you then," laughed his father.

1.  The man said to his son that you can come to the game with me tomorrow, as long as you clean the car first.

2.  The boy replied that when I was older, I cleaned the car and drove it.

3.  He added that he might let him go to the game with me.

4.  His father said that he will be too old and embarrassing for you then.

## Exercise 23: Direct/Indirect Speech

Reconstruct a conversation from the following indirect speech.

> The old woman complained that she was too tired to go to the market the following day. Her friend said that it would do her good to go, but that if she didn't feel up to it, she should stay in bed. She added that all her other friends would like to see her, since she hadn't been at the market for the previous three weeks. The old woman sighed and said that she would think about it and tell her friend later that night if she would be going.

## Exercise 24: Grammatical Gender and pronouns

For those whose first language contains grammatical gender, i.e. masculine and feminine (and perhaps neuter) nouns which do not necessarily refer to living things, this exercise will be particularly helpful. Replace the underlined nouns in the following sentences with the corresponding pronoun from the list.

| | |
|---|---|
| he/him/his | she/her |
| it/its | they/them/their |

1. The bartender placed <u>the glasses</u> on the bar.

2. The young girl smiled at her cat and gave <u>the cat</u> some milk.

3. <u>The ship</u> hit an iceberg in the North Atlantic and sank.

4. The structure of the essay is good but <u>the essay's</u> focus is unclear.

5. The moon came from behind the clouds and he saw <u>the ghost</u> again.

6. Take these letters and throw <u>the letters</u> into the fire.

7. I think <u>the weather</u> will be sunny tomorrow.

8. When the boys saw their sister, they threw <u>the doll</u> into the pool.

9. <u>The baby</u> is crying—get some toys and take <u>the toys</u> up to the nursery.

10. <u>My mother and father</u> like to take trips to exotic lands; <u>my parents</u> take <u>these trips</u> when the weather is cold at home.

## Exercise 25: Indefinite Article

Insert the correct form of the indefinite article in the following sentences.

1. I am _____ unhappy man because of my serious illness.

2. There is _____ big ostrich sleeping in the field over there.

3. We hired someone else—it was _____ unanimous decision.

4. Get me _____ inexpensive flight, and book me into _____ hotel near the harbour.

5. You need to work hard on this test, because you got _____ "F" on the last one.

## Exercise 26: Definite Article

Articles do not exist in many languages, such as **Polish, Japanese,** and **Russian.** In others, like **Farsi** and **Cantonese,** articles can be omitted. **Arabic,** on the other hand, often uses articles in greater quantities than in English. For speakers of all languages, some practice in using the definite article correctly can be useful. In the following sentences, omit or retain the definite article as appropriate.

1. I would like to order the following compact discs from the music club.

2. The advances in the computer technology make the desktop publishing easier.

3. The prices of the houses these days are beyond the reach of the newly-married couples.

4. Unlike so many guides to the travel and the sightseeing, the book I bought takes a practical approach with lots of the good advice.

5. I like to watch the films, especially the old ones with the actors like James Stewart.

## Exercise 27: Plural Nouns

Make corrections to the following sentences.

1. Walking past the park, I could hear the childs playing.

2. All the wifes went out to buy their husbands new briefs.

3. I have worked for many years in a number of dairys and factorys.

4. All four of my son-in-laws take three spoonfuls of sugar in their coffee.

5. This data is the single most important criteria in analyzing the effects of the chemical on the mouses' respiratory systems.

6. None of the private members' bills have become law yet during this session of Parliament.

7. Did you see the group of woodpeckers that has congregated outside your window?

8. The striking workers raised their fist in anger.

9. The taxidermist had a range of stuffed animals on display: four salmons, two sheeps, two gooses, and a pair of hyena's.

10. I had to write two major thesis to get my degree.

## Exercise 28: From Singular to Plural

Change the following sentences from singular to plural. Change all nouns, verbs, and pronouns as appropriate.

1. The girl is chasing her friend through a park.

2. The charity to which I give an annual donation is in serious trouble.

3. You seem to be unable to make any sense of that document.

4. I know someone in that village beyond the high mountain range who speaks a strange language.

5. A beautiful picture of that ox is hanging above my brother's bed.

6. This one is mine!

7. My teacher told me I was working too hard on my homework.

8. She should visit an old friend and have some fun.

## Exercise 29: Personal Pronouns

Make corrections to the following sentences, removing unnecessary pronouns.

1. It looks like the sun it is beginning to shine.

2. The Prime Minister and his cabinet, they are meeting at a secret location today.

3. My friend, a man who is loyal, trustworthy, and conscientious, he is also very funny.

4. Some of the eggs I bought I have already broken them.

5. The students of mine who wrote the wonderful papers on the history and role of the dramatic festivals in ancient Greece they are extremely intelligent.

## Exercise 30: Possessive Pronouns

Remember that English, unlike languages such as **French** and **Spanish**, does not use the definite article "the" before possessive pronouns like "mine" and "theirs." Other languages—**Polish** and **Russian** among them—do not have different forms for possessive pronouns and adjectives. In the exercise below, respond to the questions using the prompt that follows it.  For example,

> **Question:**  Is this your vehicle? [she]
> **Answer:**  No, it is hers.

1.   Is this your jacket? [I]

2.   Are these Mike's tools? [Dave]

3.   Is that their own truck? [we]

4.   Whose is the dog outside with the annoying bark? [you]

5.   With whose help did you build your house? [he]

6.   Were those my ideas that you included in that report? [she]

## Exercise 31: Relative Pronouns

In English, the choice of relative pronoun depends more on a human/non-human distinction than on gender or number. As in other languages, there is some distinction between subject and object, although the object relative pronoun can often be omitted.  Combine the following pairs of sentences, choosing the appropriate form of relative pronoun.

1.   There is the author. The author wrote a terrible novel.

2.   Who bought the bicycle?  The bicycle had been on my mind for weeks.

3.   You stole the money.  The widow was saving the money for a trip to Vancouver.

4.   Go and speak to the man. I gave the details to the man.

5.   These are the ties. I was going to buy the ties for you last week.

6.   Those are the finishing touches for the cake.  You've been working on them for hours.

## Exercise 32: Relative Clauses

Remember that a relative pronoun should follow as closely as possible the antecedent to which it refers.  The following sentences are confusing or ridiculous; make some changes to improve them.

1. I have been subscribing to four magazines for many years now that I never seem to read.

2. Last week, she went riding her friend's horse that she's known since her high school days.

3. Did you really like the book's cover that was sitting on the coffee table?

4. The police found the villains' getaway car that robbed the bank last Monday.

5. Let me describe for you the scene in the play I'm going to talk about at the conference.

## Exercise 33: Adjectives

Some of the sentences below are correct, while others involve an incorrect use of an adjective. Make the necessary corrections to those that require them.

1. The sky on that long summer night was crimson red.

2. The fighting in the streets was bloody and vicious, and the commotion was much.

3. When we got to the secluded resort, the interruptions and other people were few.

4. At the art gallery, the exhibits were like the exhibitors: many and varied.

5. I'd like to make a reservation for dinner tonight; we are ten.

## Exercise 34: Comparative and Superlative Adjectives

Complete the following sentences with the correct comparative or superlative form of the adjective.

1. Jason is good at French, Helga is _____, but Ivor is the _____.

2. Your eyes are much _____ than mine. [blue]

3. Her face may be pretty, but in my opinion, her sense is humour is _____. [beautiful]

4.  Of the two cars that I saw today, the hatchback was the
    _____. [expensive]

5.  You think that's bad? You should see my place—it's _____!

6.  Which of the three samples that I sent you is _____ for your
    function? [suitable]

7.  This is the _____ snow I've ever seen. [deep]

8.  We've tried all the computer systems, and have decided that your
    company's package is the _____ [easy] to learn and the
    _____. [efficient]

## Exercise 35: Adverbs

Place an adverb of your choice in the correct place in the following sentences.

1.  Make sure that you dry the dishes before you put them away.

2.  I am going to take this jewellery that I found to the police.

3.  The central bank rate has fallen over the last few weeks.

4.  When you called, I was getting dressed.

5.  He went off to university and made friends.

6.  I am reading this book so I can get on to the next one.

## Exercise 36: Adjectives vs. Adverbs

Someone has composed the following sentences and has attempted to use adverbs. Make any necessary changes so that the sentences are improved.~

1.  He played real good during the game yesterday.

2.  Everyone laughed because the teacher spelled the word wrong on
    the blackboard.

3.  The sprinter ran very fast and got to the tape before everyone else.

4.  She had to get help because she couldn't read or write proper.

5.  The researcher copied the notes very careful into his notebook.

6.   They seldom go to the ballet any more.

## Exercise 37: Prepositions

Fill in the correct preposition, or leave blank if no preposition is needed.

1.   My father was very angry _____me when I did not do what he had asked me to.

2.   We should arrive _____Denver in time for dinner.

3.   The three of them were chased _____from school.

4.   The group departed _____Paris in the early morning.

5.   We discussed _____the problem with him for a whole afternoon.

6.   We were told to continue _____ our work.

7.   We must refer _____to the first chapter to find the most important clue to the protagonist's identity.

8.   The geopolitical situation in late 1938 was different _____ what it had been only a few months earlier.

9.   He asked me what type _____VCR we wanted.

10.   She is convinced that this brand of detergent is superior _____that one.

## Exercise 38: Phrasal Verbs

In the following, replace the underlined word with a pronoun, adjusting the word order if necessary.

1.   I'm going to take up golf next summer.

2.   See if you can jump over the boxes.

3.   Speeding down the country lane, the car ran over two skunks.

4.   Give me a call and tell me what brought about this sudden change of heart.

5.   Put down the glasses before you break them.

## Exercise 39: Conjunctions

Fill in *but, although, however, despite, because* or *as a result*. Pay close attention to the punctuation.

1.   _____ he was sick, he could not come to work yesterday.

2.   _____ he was sick, he came to work yesterday.

3.   He was sick yesterday. _____, he still came to work.

4.   _____ his sickness, he still came to work yesterday.

5.   He was sick yesterday. _____, he did not come to work.

6.   He was sick yesterday, _____ he still came to work.

7.   She has practised for many long hours. _____, she is now a good player.

8.   She has practised for many long hours, _____ she is still not a good player.

9.   She is now a good player _____ she has practised for many long hours.

10.   _____ she has practised for many long hours, she is not yet a good player.

11.   She has practised for many long hours. _____, she is not yet a good player.

12.   _____ her long hours of practice, she is not yet a good player.

## Exercise 40: Easily confused words

Choose the correct word or expression.

1.   Do you think your action will have any _____[effect/affect]?

2.   The shopkeeper did not want to _____[accept/except] a credit card.

3.   The tape recording _____[compliments/complements] the study guide.

4. The _____[council/counsel] deliberated for seven hours before reaching a decision.

5. One approach is to break down the questionnaire results by age and sex. _____[Alternately/Alternatively], we may study the variations among different income levels.

6. He is very conservative and would never wish to _____[flout/flaunt] the university administration.

7. The stage can be _____[dissembled/disassembled] within two hours. (390)

8. The two elements must be seen as entirely _____[discreet/discrete].

9. She told me _____[definitely/definitively] that she would not support the motion.

10. Britain is considering whether or not to restore_____ [capitol/capital] punishment. (368)

11. The majority believe that theft is _____ [amoral/immoral] in any circumstances.

12. No politician is _____[adverse/averse] to publicity.

13. They were eager to declare the amount as a _____ capitol/capital gain.

14. The company always purchases _____ [stationary / stationery] in bulk.

15. The book is laden with a preface, a _____ [foreword / forward] and an introduction.

16. They could not gain _____ [access/excess] to the house because of the expensive security system.

17. I could not respond to your letter because it was almost _____ [eligible/illegible].

18. The retirement home has a set of strict rules which are very _____ [prescriptive/proscriptive].

19. She recently retired from her position as one of the ballet company's

_____ [principal/principle] dancers.

20. _____ [Its/It's] a miracle that the dog was able to find _____ [it's/its] way home.

## Exercise 41: More easily confused words

Once again, choose the correct word from those in brackets.

1.  The new secretary was _____ [anxious/eager] to start his new job because he had never worked for an accountant before.

2.  The next chapter is _____ [composed/comprised] of a survey of the major theorists in the field.

3.  The solar eclipse truly was an _____ [incredible/incredulous] sight.

4.  _____ [Meantime/Meanwhile], in the other room, our parents were involved in another heated discussion.

5.  The recording officer _____ [respectfully/respectively] submitted the minutes for scrutiny.

6.  I could not understand how anyone could be so insensitive and devoid of _____ [apathy/empathy/sympathy].

7.  Because she had come to the conference unprepared, Nicole could not _____ [partake/participate] in the discussion.

8.  In his _____ [later/latter] symphonies, Mozart is at the peak of his genius.

9.  I can pick him out in a crowd anywhere—he has such a _____ [distinct/distinctive] voice.

10. Many people are now choosing _____ [abstention/abstinence] as a safe _____ [alternate/alternative] to the risk of contracting AIDS.

11. Your prose is too wordy—try being more _____ [economic/economical] with your vocabulary.

12. The _____ [extent/extend] to which this can be proven is unclear from the present data.

13. It is my _____ [belief/believe] that you should _____ [practice/practise] what you preach.

14. We really enjoyed the play, and were moved by the _____ [tragic/tragical] ending.

15. I am trying to _____ that I can be adequately _____d under this policy. Can you _____ me of that? [assure/ensure/insure]

## Exercise 42: Usage

Correct the following sentences.

1. Please do not do any changes before you have asked me about them.

2. There are less people in Sweden than there are in the city of New York.

3. The college would like to increase the places available in residence.

4. According to science, it is impossible to travel faster than the speed of light.

5. Let's find a bar—I have really thirsty.

6. I know to play the bassoon, which is a valuable skill when parties get boring.

7. The headmaster has been waiting for you since ten minutes.

8. The European powers wanted to colonize Africa because of the following reasons.

9. He often forgets his office key at home.

10. He is opposed against legalizing abortion.

## Exercise 43: Affixes

Make the necessary corrections to the affixes in the sentences that follow.

1. The employee could not get over the difficultness of the training program.

2. I completed the project poorly because I disunderstood the instruc-

tions.

3. His actions were inexpected and completely unrational.

4. I have been feeling listless and inert recently, so I'm going to the doctor so that he can prescribe something to make me listful and ert again.

5. The firemen were trying out some new firefighting gear that was waterproof and inflammable.

6. She has been named as a correspondent in the divorce case.

7. People who have not kept up with changes in technology will have to be reeducated.

8. In order to reestablish himself as a respectable citizen, he has disassociated himself from his former criminal coconspirators.

## Exercise 44: Two words or one?

Choose the appropriate word (or words!) from the options in brackets.

1. Simply make the changes on the screen, and then it's _____ [already/all ready] to be printed.

2. The bank manager had _____ [a lot/alot] of concerns about my current overdraft situation on the phone today, but I assured him that I would go _____ [into/in to] see him tomorrow.

3. You _____ [maybe/may be] right that this is a _____ [straight forward/straightforward] assignment, but then again, _____ [maybe/may be] you're wrong.

4. _____ knows that _____ of your "antiques" is less than five years old. [everyone/every one]

5. One should not subject _____ [oneself/one's self] to such unpleasantness _____ [forever/for ever].

## Exercise 45: Infinitive or Gerund?

Fill in the correct choice:

1. Mr. Carruthers accused me _____[to have laughed/of laughing] at him behind his back.

2.  He has a tendency _____[to speak/of speaking] before he has thought about what effect his words may have.

3.  Mary is certainly capable _____[to get/of getting] an 'A' in this course.

4.  He has often tried to discourage me _____[to try/from trying] to get into Medical School.

5.  They seemed _____[as if they were/to be] about to attack us.

6.  The Press suspected the senator [to have been involved/of having been involved] in a conflict of interest.

## Exercise 46: Sentence Fragments and Comma Splices

In the following sentences, the incorrect punctuation has been used. Make the necessary changes.

1.  Another positive element is that outside firms will bring new or substantially revitalized agricultural resources into use, they will create new employment to operate the production facilities.

2.  Hydrochloric acid is a very dangerous substance. So always handle it very carefully.

3.  The author states his views on the difference between the two very clearly. One being strong and physical, the other weak and inadequate.

4.  The freedom fighter spun around just in time, then he fired quickly.

5.  I had to work in the most adverse weather conditions: blowing snow and a severe wind chill. Which made the job much harder.

6.  It took three hours to get to the hospital, it will take even longer to get the tests done.

## Exercise 47: The Comma

Insert commas in the appropriate places in the sentences that follow.

1.  Although the presidential race was a bitter one the transfer of power was done very amicably.

2. The essence of my whole argument however lies in the inability of the administration to protect its employees.

3. My brother the manager of the firm had the unpleasant task of firing several people.

4. I had no trouble killing the snake which incidentally was one of the smallest most insignificant snakes I have ever seen.

5. She could always rely on the support of her best friend who had been through rough times herself.

## Exercise 48: Possession and the Apostrophe

In the following sentences, correct any misuses of the apostrophe.

1. All three groups of parents attended their infant's one month paediatric checkup, and observations were made of father's interactions with their infants.

2. I would like to do an independent study on Dicken's novels.

3. The director's of the condominium corporation car is always improperly parked.

4. My three dog's dishes lie side by side, and my cat's basket is located nearby.

5. The church brethrens' greatest joy came with the reinstatement of their preacher.

6. Heracles's reputation was one of heroism, sexual conquests, and gluttony.

7. The tops of the tables' were covered with spilt beer, old peanuts, and the waitresses' generous tips.

8. When I'm proud of him, he's my brother, but when I'm not, he's my mother's and father's younger son.

9. Please do'nt make such a noise—it hurt's my ear's.

10. You should'nt say this is your friend's faults when the responsibility is your's, not their's.

## Exercise 49: Capitalization

Correct the faulty capitalization in the sentences that follow.

1.  i am planning to visit spain next Summer.

2.  The newspaper reported that doctor Smith was planning to climb mount Everest in june.

3.  The Captains and Sergeants were visiting the Professors last monday, but i noticed that Professor Valdez was not there.

4.  It is not the policy of the university to tolerate academic dishonesty.

5.  While on a boating trip in Rice lake, the students read their wet copies of John Braine's <u>Room At The Top</u>.

6.  Regardless of one's feelings about god and the bible, the power of the Story of Jesus and other Biblical tales cannot be underestimated.

## Exercise 50: Word Order

Make the necessary changes to the word order of the following sentences.

Improve the word order in the following sentences.

1.  This can be the result either of natural events or human actions.

2.  In the end, Hitler neither conquered Britain nor the Soviet Union.

3.  We should first ask what are the conditions under which an electronics industry is likely to flourish.

4.  Passions can interfere either sporadically on particular occasions, or they can be a continual influence on one's actions.

5.  The conclusions we draw will be largely determined by what are the assumptions we start with.

6.  The Tiger supporters in the crowd were few.

7.  The books I lent to my friend, I need them back soon.

8.  The men who are responsible for installing the joists, the supervisor wanted to see them.

9. He neither wants pity nor charity.

10. They were given sentences of between one and three years all except those who had not committed any violent offenses.

11. I and my friends usually spend holidays together.

12. In this class there are three students only.

13. I asked Faith how was she feeling.

14. My father asked me what was I doing.

15. They asked us what was wrong?

# PART II: General Diagnostic and Language Specific Exercises

This section is designed to be a general diagnostic review of particular errors, and is structured to focus on those errors made by speakers of particular languages or language groups. However, speakers of all languages would benefit from the added practice offered by these exercises. In each passage, make any corrections that seem appropriate, and then propose changes to the passages to improve their style.

### Exercise 51: General Exercise A

Of particular help to speakers of Oriental and Far Eastern languages.

When I was work in a factory in home country, I like this job because there are many machines for me to work. It was difficult to felt a sense of the morale because the important decision of company could not made the employees. The manager should make effort in communicate with the workers to find out that whether they in need of something. People they always so inspired by the interest of their employer. The success and the productivity is therefore increase. I can't remembered anytime when my boss he come to me to ask me the question. I would liked that he come so that I can tell to him about the effectiveness and the productivity. But he not come so I go to another company. There I get good reward for that I do. If I am well done on the job, I am reward with the money and the praise. My grandmother think the young people all they want is money. There are something more than money and can not buy by money. They are include friendship and love. This is right but I still like the money.

[adapted from student's paper]

## Exercise 52: General Exercise B

Of particular help to speakers of Slavic languages.

Since 1990 I have a dog which is called Maggie. I never not like to stay too long away from house because, she waits on me there. You saw my dog, yes? I think you saw her when I was yesterday to office. She most white and most beautiful dog I never seen. Once, when I in the country with Maggie, someone which I never saw previously caught her and said to me with anger that she is his dog and wants her, but I to him said this dog is my! This story then was not funny, but these days I am laughing to it. However, I never again will not be careless with dog because she to me very precious. That what I want, it is to always her love and protect so that she for always would be as friend to me. To me difficult, to imagine the life without her, although before I am living much year without no dog.

## Exercise 53: General Exercise C

Of particular help to speakers of Romance languages (French, Italian, Portuguese, Spanish).

When I was more young than am now, was swimming a lot in the lake which was being near to the home of my family. I thought me to be a good swimmer, and I went to this lake even when the weather was being very cold. I was it calling the my lake, and the people were coming me to see there, more than to the my house. Sometimes I never not wanted to leave that place, especially in warm and light nights in summer. I never was so very happy that I was then; wanted that I could there to stay forever. The water she was warm, and I felt me refreshing and calm. My parents saw me to swim and to be the girl the most happy of the world. Today my children also likes to swim, and the my husband and me we them take to that lake for to visit my mother and my father (the grandparents of my children) which are now retired. They take a boat small into the lake from which the children they jump of its edge. They splash and laugh—I know them to be as happy as me. Especially my son, who has only five, he likes to swim. Already he is very strong. But when he has hunger and wants to eat, soon he gets him out the lake, dries him, puts the clothes, and eats his food favourites...some apples and little of chocolate.

## Exercise 54: General Exercise D

A general review exercise for everyone. In this exercise, some words are used wrongly; in other instances, there is a choice of words to fill the blank. Enjoy it, because it's the last exercise in the book!

Languages _____ [is/are] always _____ [notorious /notoriously] difficult subject to study. It is infact possible to study in order that you _____ [improve/to improve] your english, or improvement does it only come through _____ [a/the] process of read and write? The body of the public opinion has swinged wildly back and forth on this issue over the _____ [past/previous] thirty year. In the 1950s and the 1960s the prevailing view _____ [among/between] educators _____ [was/were] that the students they were being _____ [contracted/constricted] by a _____ [accessive/excessive] emphasis on _____ [correctness/correctivity] over _____ [creativeness/creativity].

_____ [Given/Giving] the experience of the seventys and the eighthys, is difficult to _____ [oppress/suppress] a smile at such grand _____ [allusions/illusions]. Language does changes, and always will there be unagreement as to _____ [various/varying] points of the usage. But the most of we has came to _____ [appreciate/depreciate] that in the _____ [coarse/course] of the _____ [passed/past] generation that the level of the communication in our society will not be rised by leaving the students that they sort _____ [out/up] english usage in there owns. Learning that certain forms of english usage are be considered to be _____ [superior/superlative] to the others, can to help to create the _____ [channells/channels] _____ [thorough/through] _____ [which/witch] the _____ [creativeness/creativity] can be _____ [best/better] exprest.

# ANSWER KEY TO EXERCISES

## Part I

**Exercise I**

1. Trains in Burma usually run on time, although it sometimes takes many hours to get from one place to another. The trip from Belowa to Rangoon, for example, lasts about eleven hours. The Railway Corporation uses several different types of locomotive—steam, electric, and diesel. The newest are the electric locomotives that travel between Rangoon and Mutisa.

2. Most of the electricity that the State needs comes from the dam. When the water flows over the large turbines, it turns them and this produces large amounts of electricity.

3. When a debate starts, the Chairman always introduces the topic and then three speakers from each team argue for or against the resolution(s). Each speaker talks for several minutes. At the end of the debate the Chairman gives anyone in the crowd who wishes to speak a chance to do so.

4. In politics as in everyday life the variations that interest us occur in two dimensions. Sometimes political scientists are curious about variations over time. For instance, they may ask why the number of votes received by the various parties fluctuates so much from one election to the next. At other times, political scientists concentrate their attention on variations over space. They may be interested, for example, in why one nation's government seems to enjoy more success than its neighbour in combatting inflation, or protecting human rights.

**Exercise 2**

(1) we play.  (2) they spend.  (3) he cooks; she reads.  (4) they listen; he/she says.

**Exercise 3**

(1) the ability ... increases.  (2) the big payoff ... comes.  (3) none of the three ... has.  (4) Typos ... which make ... have been made.

## Exercise 4

(1) rises; sets; think; revolves; is; circles; shines; is. (2) follows; comes; asks; introduces; talks; assigns; finish; corrects; are; tells. (3) is; sympathize; are made; accuses; says; seems.

## Exercise 5

(1) are. (2) are; are. (3) are. (4) is. (5) is. (6) is; are.

## Exercise 6

(1) are fighting; appears; is going on; is interfering. (2) rings; answer; am feeling; put; am not answering. (3) returns; are hiding; wants; kills; kills. (4) am looking for; hate; expects/is expecting; is trying. (5) is taking off; take off; land; are; bet; are arriving; departing; like; am looking forward.

## Exercise 7

(1) have been working. (2) have been. (3) have been looking for. (4) has not taught. (5) have not talked. (6) has been playing. (7) have been trying; has been hiding. (8) For how many years have you been following ...?

## Exercise 8

(1) have written; wrote. (2) has disappeared. (3) exercised; have not exercised. (4) got; has not got. (5) has copied; gave; came. (6) have not been able; fell.

## Exercise 9

(1) came; left. (2) asked; said/had said. (3) arrived; found out; had happened. (4) arrived; had never seen. (5) had not read; went. (6) married; knew; had had. (7) had eaten; came. (8) had tried; hit.

## Exercise 10

(1) will have painted; return. (2) are; will be able. (3) will have done; get up. (4) win; will quit; travel. (5) will stop; stop. (6) will celebrate; finish.

## Exercise 11

(1) would return. (2) will return. (3) would find. (4) will find. (5) will take. (6) would you do. (7) will be. (8) would buy. (9) see. (10) win. (11) won. (12) worked. (13) works. (14) came. (15) promise. (16) arranged. (17)

would live; smoked.

## Exercise 12

(1) will supply; pay; have. (2) replies; will be able. (3) believed; would go; is. (4) go; will take. (5) had arrived. (6) had not been hiding; would have been assembled; would have lost. (7) had planted. (8) would have done. (9) had asked. (10) would probably not have sunk.

## Exercise 14

(1) were. (2) was. (3) leave. (4) are. (5) be.

## Exercise 15

1.  I do not believe in allowing children to decide what they should do in the classroom because it does not let then become more independent.

2.  Caffeine in coffee is not more powerful than caffeine found in tea; if given the choice, I would not drink coffee.

3.  If I were not able to see without my glasses, I could not wear regular sunglasses when I am driving.

4.  Ted did not play rugby when he was young because he did not think it would make him fit and strong.

5.  If the orchestra did not play quietly, the opera singers would not be able to be heard clearly.

## Exercise 16

1.  We don't know of any way we can get around the problem.

2.  I cannot ever get to know her because she never says anything to anybody in class.

3.  No library services are available today because of the holiday.

4.  Don't repeat a word of this to anybody!

5.  She hardly does anything when she is not constantly supervised.

6.  Neither of her sons could read or write anything.

## Exercise 17

1. Is the lava flowing very quickly down the side of the volcano?

2. Were the people in the villages afraid that a major eruption would happen soon?

3. Do you expect the year ahead to be more prosperous?

4. Did the weight of the dictionaries cause the shelf to break?

5. Do you eat clams and squid at least three times a week?

6. Do I look like your brother?

## Exercise 18

1. How often is your car serviced?
   Tell me how often your car is serviced.

2. What is the best way to get rid of mice?
   Tell me what the best way is to get rid of mice.

3. Where does the sun appear to rise in mid-June?
   Tell me where the sun appears to rise in mid-June.

4. Which shirt do you prefer?
   Tell me which shirt you prefer.

5. Why do people like to ski?
   Tell me why people like to ski.

6. Who was Britain's first female Prime Minister?
   Tell me who Britain's first female Prime Minister was.

## Exercise 19

(1) aren't they?  (2) is he?  (3) will I?  (4) are you?  (5) doesn't it? (or don't they?)  (6) didn't they?

## Exercise 20

(possible solutions)

1. His wife waved to him from the sidewalk when he was riding the bus to work.

2. When it is covered with aluminum siding, we will have a much more saleable house.

3. An increase in taxes will be required if the deficit is to be reduced.

4. The implications of Smith's argument are that he allows us to justify our selfish behaviour.

5. Having covered the issue of stratification, I will deal with the means of distributing income next.

6. A few examples should suffice to give a sense of the density of structuralist prose.

7. We have asked for a random survey of the attitudes of consumers.

8. There is no doubt—if we consider all of this evidence—that an increased awareness of the usefulness of uniform and objectively-defined time led to the spread of clocks, and not the other way round.

9. Although he was widely regarded as a failure by observers at the time, we can now see that Truman was a remarkably successful president.

10. Faulkner's novel is written from several points of view.

## Exercise 21

1. She can do whatever she chooses.

2. The book is well written and beautifully laid out.

3. He says that he rang me over the phone.

4. They have stolen everything I own.

5. This blouse shrank when I washed it in hot water.

6. The ship sank in a hundred metres of water.

(1) chose; was. (2) drank. (3) burst. (4) fell; lay. (5) fled; saw. (6) forgave. (7) ground. (8) laid; forgot. (9) lent. (10) rang. (11) sought. (12) shone. (13) shot. (14) shrank. (15) sang. (16) sank; were. (17) slid. (18) spent. (19) spun; went. (20) spat. (21) split. (22) sprang. (23) swam. (24) wept; heard. (25) wound. (26) wrung.

## Exercise 22

1. The man said to his son that he could go to the game with him the following day, as long as he cleaned the car first.

2. The boy replied that when he became older, he would be cleaning the car and driving it himself.

3. He added that he might let his father go to the game with him.

4. His father said that he would be too old and embarrassing for him then.

## Exercise 23

**Old Woman:** "I am too tired to go to the market tomorrow."

**Friend:** "It will do you good to go, but if you don't feel up to it, you should stay in bed. All your other friends would like to see you, since you've not been at the market for the last three weeks."

**Old Woman:** "Oh well, I'll think about it and tell you tonight if I'm going or not."

## Exercise 24

(1) them. (2) it. (3) she/it. (4) its. (5) it. (6) them. (7) it. (8) they; her; it. (9) he/she; them. (10) they; they; them.

## Exercise 25

(1) an. (2) a. (3) a. (4) an; a/an. (5) an.

## Exercise 26

1. I would like to order the following compact discs from the music club.

2. Advances in computer technology make desktop publishing easier.

3. Prices of houses these days are beyond the reach of newly-married couples.

4. Unlike so many guides to travel and sightseeing, the book I bought takes a practical approach with lots of good advice.

5. I like to watch films, especially (the) old ones with actors like James

Stewart.

## Exercise 27

(1) children. (2) wives. (3) dairies; factories. (4) sons-in-law; spoonsful. (5) These data are the single most important criterion in analyzing the effects of the chemical on the mice's respiratory systems. (6) has become law. (7) have congregated. (8) fists. (9) salmon; sheep; geese; hyenas. (10) theses.

## Exercise 28

1. The girls are chasing their friends through some parks.

2. The charities to which we give annual donations are in serious trouble.

3. You seem to be unable to make any sense of those documents.

4. We know some people in those villages beyond the high mountain ranges who speak strange languages.

5. Beautiful pictures of those oxen are hanging above our brothers' beds.

6. These ones are ours!

7. Our teachers told us we were working too hard on our homework.

8. They should visit some old friends and have some fun.

## Exercise 29

1. It looks like the sun is beginning to shine.

2. The Prime Minister and his cabinet are meeting at a secret location today.

3. My friend, a man who is loyal, trustworthy, and conscientious, is also very funny.

4. Some of the eggs I bought I have already broken.

5. The students of mine who wrote the wonderful papers on the history and role of the dramatic festivals in ancient Greece are extremely intelligent.

## Exercise 30

(1) No, it is mine. (2) No, they are Dave's. (3) No, it is ours. (4) It is yours. (5) With his help. (6) No, they were hers.

## Exercise 31

1.   There is the author who/that wrote a terrible novel.

2.   Who bought the bicycle that had been on my mind for weeks?

3.   You stole the money (that) the widow was saving for a trip to Vancouver.

4.   (Formal) Go and speak to the man to whom I gave the details. (Informal) Go and speak to the man that I gave the details to.

5.   These are the ties (that) I was going to buy for you last week.

6.   Those are the finishing touches for the cake (that) you've been working on for hours.

## Exercise 32

1.   I have been subscribing to four magazines for many years now, and I never seem to read them.

2.   Last week, she went riding a horse that belongs to a friend that she's known since her high school days.

3.   Did you really like the cover of the book that was sitting on the coffee table?

4.   The police found the getaway car that the villains who robbed the bank last Monday used.

5.   Let me describe for you the scene I'm going to talk about at the conference.

## Exercise 33

2.   The fighting in the streets was bloody and vicious, and there was much commotion.

3.   When we got to the secluded resort, there were few interruptions and few people too.

5.    I'd like to make a reservation for dinner tonight; there are ten of us.

## Exercise 34

(1) better; best.  (2) bluer.  (3) more beautiful.  (4) more/less expensive.  (5) worse.  (6) the most suitable.  (7) deepest.  (8) easiest; most efficient.

## Exercise 35 (possible answers)

1.    Make sure that you dry the dishes properly before you put them away.

2.    I am going to take this jewellery that I found to the police right away.

3.    The central bank rate has fallen steadily over the last few weeks.

4.    When you called, I was hurriedly getting dressed.

5.    He went off to university and immediately made friends.

6.    I am reading this book quickly so I can get on to the next one.

## Exercise 36

1.    He played really well during the game yesterday.

2.    Everyone laughed because the teacher spelled the word wrongly on the blackboard.

3.    The sprinter ran very fast and got to the tape before everyone else.

4.    She had to get help because she couldn't read or write properly.

5.    The researcher copied the notes very carefully into his notebook.

6.    They seldom go to the ballet any more.

## Exercise 37

(1) with.  (2) in.  (3) away.  (4) from.  (5) no preposition.  (6) with, or no preposition.  (7) no additional preposition.  (8) from/to.  (9) of.  (10) to.

## Exercise 38

1.    I'm going to take it up next summer.

2.  See if you can jump over them.

3.  Speeding down the country lane, the car ran them over (<u>or</u> over them).

4.  Give me a call and tell me what brought this about.

5.  Put them down before you break them.

## Exercise 39

(1) because. (2) although. (3) however. (4) despite. (5) as a result. (6) but. (7) as a result. (8) but. (9) because. (10) although. (11) however. (12) despite.

## Exercise 40

(1) effect. (2) accept. (3) complements. (4) council. (5) alternatively. (6) flout. (7) disassembled. (8) discrete. (9) definitively. (10) capital. (11) immoral. (12) averse. (13) capital. (14) stationery. (15) foreword. (16) access. (17) illegible. (18) proscriptive. (19) principal. (20) it's; its.

## Exercise 41

(1) eager. (2) comprised. (3) incredible. (4) meanwhile. (5) respectfully. (6) empathy. (7) participate. (8) later. (9) distinctive. (10) abstinence; alternative. (11) economical. (12) extent. (13) belief; practise. (14) tragic. (15) ensure; insured; assure.

## Exercise 42

1.  Please do not make any changes before you have asked me about them.

2.  There are fewer people in Sweden than there are in the city of New York.

3.  The college would like to increase the number of places available in residence.

4.  Scientists hold that it is impossible to travel faster than the speed of light.

5.  Let's find a bar—I am really thirsty.

6. I can play the bassoon, which is a valuable skill when parties get boring.

7. The headmaster has been waiting for you for ten minutes.

8. The European powers wanted to colonize Africa for the following reasons.

9. He often leaves his office key at home.

10. He is opposed to legalizing abortion.

## Exercise 43

1. The employee could not get over the difficulty of the training program.

2. I completed the project poorly because I misunderstood the instructions.

3. His actions were unexpected and completely irrational.

4. I have been feeling listless and inert recently, so I'm going to the doctor so that he can prescribe something to make me feel more lively and active again.

5. The firemen were trying out some new firefighting gear that was waterproof and non-inflammable (or non-flammable).

6. She has been named as a co-respondent in the divorce case.

7. People who have not kept up with changes in technology will have to be re-educated.

8. In order to re-establish himself as a respectable citizen, he has dissociated himself from his former criminal co-conspirators.

## Exercise 44

(1) all ready. (2) a lot; in to. (3) may be; straightforward; maybe. (4) everyone; every one. (5) oneself; forever.

## Exercise 45

(1) of laughing. (2) to speak. (3) of getting. (4) from trying. (5) to be. (6) of having been involved.

## Exercise 46

1. Another positive element is that outside firms will bring new or substantially revitalized agricultural resources into use. They will create new employment to operate the production facilities.

2. Hydrochloric acid is a very dangerous substance, so always handle it very carefully.

3. The author states his views on the difference between the two very clearly: one is strong and physical, the other weak and inadequate.

4. The freedom fighter spun around just in time, and then he fired quickly.

5. I had to work in the most adverse weather conditions: blowing snow and a severe wind chill. This made the job much harder.

6. It took three hours to get to the hospital; it will take even longer to get the tests done.

## Exercise 47

1. Although the presidential race was a bitter one, the transfer of power was done very amicably.

2. The essence of my whole argument, however, lies in the inability of the administration to protect its employees.

3. My brother, the manager of the firm, had the unpleasant task of firing several people.

4. I had no trouble killing the snake, which, incidentally, was one of the smallest, most insignificant snakes I have ever seen.

5. She could always rely on the support of her best friend, who had been through rough times herself.

## Exercise 48

1. All three groups of parents attended their infants' one month paediatric checkup, and observations were made of fathers' interactions with their infants.

2. I would like to do an independent study on Dickens's novels.

3. The director of the condominium corporation's car is always improperly parked.

4. My three dogs' dishes lie side by side, and my cat's basket is located nearby.

5. The church brethren's greatest joy came with the reinstatement of their preacher.

6. Herakles' reputation was one of heroism, sexual conquests, and gluttony.

7. The tops of the tables were covered with spilt beer, old peanuts, and the waitresses' generous tips.

8. When I'm proud of him, he's my brother, but when I'm not, he's my mother and father's younger son.

9. Please don't make such a noise—it hurts my ears.

10. You shouldn't say this is your friends' fault when the responsibility is yours, not theirs.

## Exercise 49

1. I am planning to visit Spain next summer.

2. The newspaper reported that Doctor Smith was planning to climb Mount Everest in June.

3. The captains and sergeants were visiting the professors last Monday, but I noticed that Professor Valdez was not there.

4. It is not the policy of the University to tolerate academic dishonesty.

5. While on a boating trip in Rice Lake, the students read their wet copies of John Braine's <u>Room at the Top</u>.

6. Regardless of one's feelings about God and the Bible, the power of the story of Jesus and other biblical tales cannot be underestimated.

## Exercise 50

1. This can be the result of either natural events or human actions.

2. In the end, Hitler conquered neither Britain nor the Soviet Union.

3. We should first ask under what conditions an electronics industry is likely to flourish.

4. Passions can either interfere sporadically on particular occasions, or they can be a continual influence on one's actions.

5. The conclusions we draw will be determined largely by what the assumptions are that we start with.

6. There were few Tiger supporters in the crowd.

7. I need the books I lent to my friend back soon.

8. The supervisor wanted to see the men that are responsible for installing the joists.

9. He wants neither pity nor charity.

10. All except those who had not committed any violent offenses were given sentences of between one and three years.

11. My friends and I usually spend holidays together.

12. There are only three students in this class.

13. I asked Faith how she was feeling.

14. My father asked me what I was doing.

15. They asked us what was wrong.

# Part II

### Exercise 51: General Exercise A

Corrected version:

When I worked in a factory in my home country, I liked the job because there were many machines for me to work. It was difficult to feel a sense of morale because the important decisions of the company could not be made by the employees. The manager should have made an effort to communicate with the workers to find out whether they were in need of anything. People are always really inspired by the interest of their employer. Success and productivity increase, therefore. I can't remember a time when my boss ever came to me to ask me a question. I would have liked him to come so that I could tell him about effectiveness and productivity. But he did not come so I went to another company. There I got good rewards for what I did. If I did well in the job, I was rewarded with money and praise. My grandmother thinks all young people want is money. There are some things more than money and these cannot be bought by money. They include friendship and love. This is right but I still like money.

Improved version:

When I worked in a factory in my home country, I liked the job because there were many machines for me to work. It was difficult to feel a sense of morale, however, because employees could not make the important decisions of the company themselves. The manager should have made an effort to communicate with the workers to find out whether they were in need of anything, because people are always really inspired by the interest of their employer. As a result, success and productivity increase. I can't remember a time when my boss ever came to me to ask me a question. I would have liked him to come so that I could tell him about effectiveness and productivity, but he did not come so I went to another company. There I got good rewards for what I did: if I did well in the job, I was rewarded with money and praise. My grandmother thinks all young people want is money. There are some things worth more than money, however, which cannot be bought by money, like friendship and love. Although I think this is right, I still like money.

## Exercise 52: General Exercise B

Corrected version:

Since 1990 I have had a dog who is called Maggie. I never like to stay away from home too long, because she waits for me there. You have seen my dog, haven't you? I think you saw her when I was at the office yesterday. She is the whitest and the most beautiful dog I have ever seen. Once, when I was in the country with Maggie, someone I had never seen before caught her and angrily said to me that she was his dog and that he wanted her, but I said to him that this dog was mine! This story was not funny then, but I laugh at it now. However, I will never again be careless with my dog because she is very precious to me. What I want is always to love and protect her so that she will always be a friend to me. It is difficult for me to imagine life without her, although before I lived for many years without a dog.

Improved version:

Since 1990 I have had a dog called Maggie. I never like to stay away from home too long, because I know she will be waiting for me to return. You've seen my dog, haven't you? I think you saw her when I was at the office yesterday. She is the whitest, most beautiful dog I have ever seen. I almost lost her once, however. One day, when I was in the country with Maggie, someone I had never seen before grabbed her and angrily said to me that she was his dog and that he wanted her, but I said to him that this dog was mine! This story was not funny then, but I laugh at it now. However, I will never again be careless with my dog because she is very precious to me. What I want is always to love and protect her so that she will always be a friend to me. It is difficult for me to imagine life without her, although before I had her I lived for many years without a dog.

## Exercise 53: General Exercise C

Corrected version:

When I was younger than I am now, I would swim a lot in the lake which was near my family's home. I thought I was a good swimmer, and I would go to that lake even when the weather was very cold. I called it my lake, and the people would come to see me there, more than to my house. Sometimes I never wanted to leave that place, especially on warm and light summer nights. I have never been so happy as I was then; I wanted to stay there forever. The water was warm, and I felt refreshed and calm. My parents saw me swimming and that I was the happiest girl in the world. Today my children also like to swim, and my husband and I take them to that lake to visit my mother and father (the grandparents of my children) who are now retired. They take a small boat into the lake from which the children jump off the edge. They splash and laugh—I know they are as happy as me. Especially my son, who is only five, likes to swim. Already he is very strong. But when he is hungry and wants to eat, he gets out of the lake, dries himself, puts on his clothes, and eats his favourite foods...apples and a little chocolate.

Improved version:

When I was a little girl, I would swim a lot in the lake near my family home. I thought I was a good swimmer, and I would go to that lake even when it was very cold. I called it "my" lake, and people would come to see me there more than they would call on me at home. Sometimes I never wanted to leave that place, especially on warm, light summer's nights. I have never been as happy as I was then; I wanted to stay there forever. The water was warm, and I felt calm and refreshed. My parents saw me swimming and knew that I was the happiest girl in the world. Today, my children also like to swim, and my husband and I take them to that lake to visit my parents (the children's grandparents) who are now retired. They all take a small boat into the lake and jump off the edge. They splash and laugh—I know they are as happy as I was. My son, especially, likes to swim. He is very strong already. However, when he is hungry, he gets out of the lake, gets dried, gets dressed, and eats his favourite foods...apples and chocolate.

## Exercise 54: General Exercise D

Languages are always notoriously difficult subjects to study. Is it, in fact, possible to study in order to improve your English, or does improvement only come through the process of reading and writing? The body of public opinion has swung wildly back and forth on this issue over the past thirty years. In the 1950s and 1960s the prevailing view among educators was that the students were being constricted by an excessive emphasis on correctness over creativity.

Given the experience of the seventies and the eighties, it is difficult to suppress a smile at such grand illusions. Language does change, and there will always be disagreement as to various points of usage. But most of us have come to appreciate that in the course of the past generation the level of communication in our society will not be raised by leaving the students to sort out English usage on their own. Learning that certain forms of English usage are considered to be superior to others can help to create the channels through which creativity can be best expressed.

# INDEX

Printed in Canada